Wholly Sober

How I stopped thinking about drinking
and started loving my life

TERESA RODDEN

.

DISCLAIMER:
The information provided in this book is based on my
life experiences. I have provided reference material
for citations and additional information. Names and
some locations have been changed to protect
individuals' identities. I limited the information shared
to what was pertinent to my story. My intention is only
to be helpful, not hurtful.
This book and the content is not intended to
diagnose or treat any medical condition, disease or
issue.

DEDICATION

Mom
I love you

CONTENTS

ACKNOWLEDGEMENTS

Chapters		Introduction	1
	1	Priming	12
	2	Disconnecting	33
	3	Defeated	55
	4	Darkness	81
	5	Doctor	106
	6	Outpatient	125
	7	Alcoholics Anonymous	147
	8	God	167
	9	Reckoning	188
	10	Love	213
	11	Letting Go	235
	12	Freedom	259
	13	Curiosity	270
		Conclusion	288

ACKNOWLEDGMENTS

Rich, my love for you extends beyond the human experience. Your patience and love through the last few years have not gone unnoticed nor underappreciated.
I love you deeply.
Sharina, my sister, my friend, my constant. Your love and words of encouragement kept me going when I wanted to stop.
Dr. Laura Crawshaw, thank you for your support and belief in me. Your wisdom, mentoring and friendship have been invaluable during this process.
Bethany Martin, cover design, thank you for listening and creating from the heart.
Christi Krug, writing coach, thank you for helping me gain the confidence to write and stretch myself through the art and magic of words.
Madeleine Eno, structural editor, thank you for helping me complete my journey with confidence.

INTRODUCTION

Hello, My name is Teresa Rodden, and I don't know if I'm an alcoholic. That's the truth.

I do know that if I had continued down the traditional path of recovery, I would have gotten drunk again.

Why am I writing this book?

Because I saw so many people struggle with the 12-steps and in the Alcoholics Anonymous rooms. Because I saw many not drinking, but still miserable, literally hanging on one meeting at a time as if hoping to find THE answer there. Because I became so hyper aware, if I had to live like that to be "sober," I would rather be drunk.

This book is not intended to bash Alcoholics Anonymous. In fact, I believe the support I received in the rooms helped me to get sober. But in a few short months, it was these same rooms that made me want to say, "Fuck it!" and get drunk.

Off I went with less than a year sober, facing what is referred to as a "disease," alone without any treatment or support.

I will share with you in more detail about how I came

to the decision to leave AA, but what's important is that I get back to why this book, why now and why me.

This book began with my dream to be on the Oprah Winfrey show.

In 2010, as a life coach with a few years of sobriety under my belt, and having gone from feeling like a toddler learning to navigate a sober life to being a confident woman with no need for alcohol or AA, I submitted an audition video for my own television show on Oprah's new OWN network. I'd dreamed of sitting with Oprah as she recognized me for some groundbreaking gift I brought to empower women and change their lives forever. And I had an important topic to examine, Women and Recovery. "Changing the Face of Recovery" was the title of my three minutes of unedited video.

I wanted to focus on what made women not want to speak of their recovery, and whisper when they did. Whereas a man wears it like a badge of honor and announces to the world, "Hi, my name is Don, and I'm a recovering alcoholic."

I wanted to interview women in recovery and

highlight all the different paths taken. I wanted to explore, discover and expose that there had to be other ways.

I wanted answers to the questions that had been dogging me for so long.

Why was I able to walk away from AA and remain sober? And at the time having seven years of sobriety without following an identifiable, as of yet, process was kind of scary. If I broke again, how would I get fixed?

I started shifting my life coaching practice from a safe "health" focus toward the more ambivalent "life recovery."

Even though I didn't have my process mapped out at the time, I felt that by offering accountability, personal success and heartfelt support, I could make a difference with women who struggled with alcohol.

I wasn't awarded the show, but doing the video established my position on sobriety: Not everyone who struggles with alcohol is alcoholic and there's more than one way to live sober.

But using the same words I'd learned to describe the

woman who struggles with alcohol, I was attracting the mindset of powerless, can't help myself, and it's-the-disease's-fault-that-I'm-miserable-and-unable-to-stay-sober women.

I don't fault them. If you do a search for books or information on problem drinking, you will quickly learn about alcoholism and read the same stories told for nearly a century. It's written as gospel, and there are plenty in the congregation of AA to vehemently support the message.

I didn't feel comfortable coaching the same twelve-step rhetoric I had walked away from, but it was the strongly held belief I kept finding through all my studies and research. Every book I opened or website I found on recovery touted the twelve steps and reaffirmed we are powerless. It was frustrating, and I felt defeated.

How could this be? Am I such an anomaly, that I could have sobriety without the struggle to abstain and not attend meetings or follow the twelve steps?

In 2011, frustrated by the lack of integrity I felt coaching women in life recovery using the methodology that caused me to run from the rooms of AA nearly a decade before, I went back to coaching what I could with less conflict--general life and health coaching.

Then in November 2012, my path changed. At the end of a weekend event, we ceremoniously gathered in a circle, and each one of us had an opportunity to make a declaration of how we were moving forward. And with tears falling, I stated I was going to help women break free from their abuse of alcohol.

Where the hell did that come from? It wasn't even on the conscious radar. But I knew. I knew right then and there it could never be anything else. I was being called by Spirit to challenge and change the thoughts, perspectives and approaches for women and alcohol.

Back to the drawing board. I sought anything that would make sense of the success I'd had without the traditional recovery steps.

I couldn't find it in the recovery world because it simply did not exist.

I knew I was the one to write it.

So I began to dissect my process.

How did I do it? How did I do the impossible? How did I manage to maintain my sobriety without meetings and twelve steps? What made my decision to quit drinking stick? How come I never struggled with not drinking?

The charges came in my mind echoing comments I'd heard in the AA rooms before:

Maybe you're not an alcoholic.

Maybe you're still going to get drunk and not be able to quit.

Maybe the monster inside is still doing push-ups and waiting to take you down.

I have since found a few books on recovery that discuss alternative paths. There are some that utilize hypnotherapy, one suggested a large amount of supplements partnered with cognitive behavioral therapy, and another offers help through pharmaceuticals. Since I didn't use any of these methods, I can't speak to their effectiveness, but I do believe AA is not the only way. And I am a huge advocate for women to be empowered with options.

I want to go on record here: I believe AA does a lot of

good and I am not opposed to it for anyone who wants to go that avenue to get help and support. I support you one hundred percent. I know plenty of people who have many years sober and attribute their sobriety to the rooms of AA and twelve steps.

But I will warn it's typically the position of the AA community that their way is the only way. When I suggest that not all problem drinkers are alcoholic and that not all alcoholics will find their peace in AA, I am accused of heresy.

The way I organized this book is my story from the beginning—from my first alcohol experience to my darkest drunken days. From the journey of out-patient and AA to ultimately navigating the path to living life successfully sober and helping other women do the same.

Throughout the pages, I share personal stories along with expert opinions, theories, science-backed studies and research that anchor the process that has gifted me sobriety for over thirteen years, to become a woman I am proud to be and live a life I am deeply grateful for.

I offer a more expansive understanding of what

sobriety really means and how it's so much different than what I was taught in the early days of seeking help for my problem drinking.

I tell my story to help women find freedom from the need to misuse alcohol and become empowered to take charge of their life.

It's the scariest thing I've done and it's also why I'm here. This is my calling.

I don't know if I'm an alcoholic. I don't identify as such.

But that doesn't matter to me.

What matters is consciously pursuing the life I want to live and becoming the woman I aspire to be.

"I am not afraid--I was born to do this."

–Joan Of Arc

PART ONE

THE STORM

The greater the difficulty the more glory in surmounting it. Skillful pilots gain their reputation from storms and tempests.

–Epictetus

CHAPTER ONE

Priming

Every book is a quotation;

and every house is a quotation out of all forests,

and mines, and stone quarries;

and every man is a quotation from all his ancestors.

–   Ralph Waldo Emerson

[1]The source of addictions is not to be found in genes, but in the early childhood environment.

Dr. Gabor Mate, *In the Realm of Hungry Ghosts*

---

[1] http://drgabormate.com/topic/addiction/

Christmas Day, 1972. I'm five years old. My head is pounding and my stomach doesn't feel so good. I'm squatted down in front of my brand-new Easy-Bake oven — it's my first hangover.

The night before, Bob showed up with a bunch of Christmas presents and a bottle of rum. Somebody had the brilliant idea to play a drinking game with the kids as we opened presents. The bigger the present, the bigger the drink we had to take.

I had the biggest present! I knew I was going to have to drink a lot to get it. The drink was kind of icky and burned my throat when I swallowed, but I kept my eye on the prize. And after a couple swallows, it didn't bother me as much. Our Snoopy's Christmas album was playing. The lights on the tree were dancing and blurring together. They were so pretty.

Bob laughed and slapped mom on the knee, "Oh, come on! It's Christmas. Lighten up. Which present do you want to open?" He winked at mom. Mom looked happy, but a little sad too. I wonder if she didn't like the taste either?

I'm not sure if getting drunk at five turned on some addiction switch or doomed me to become a drunk, but it certainly delivered the message that alcohol is okay and can be fun. And it makes Christmas lights dance.

I come from a lineage of women who could and would consume near their weight in booze.

My Mother, Judy

Beer was Mom's drink of choice. And her personality would shift almost with every one.

Beers 1-3: She was happy, free and loosened up. Elvis Presley would come out of the album slip and onto the turntable. Mom would sway and smile singing the words. You could almost see her transporting herself in to another time. This was the way I wished Mom always was. Instead of always so worried and bitchy.

Beers 4-6: If she had a bone to pick with anyone, this was picking time. Bob was often her target. "You fucking faggot. Mother-fucking queer." I don't know that she really understood what those words meant, as much as she knew they pissed him off.

Beers 7-8: She was so sorry, accompanied with tears

and snot. Picking up the phone and drunk-dialing, she could reach people far and wide. Slurring her words and repeating her grievances with Elvis singing about being lonely tonight in the background. When you answered calls back then without caller ID, you prayed it wasn't Judy calling drunk.

After that, she cycled through emotions with no way to predict what was next. Eventually finding her way out the door. We never knew what the night would bring—arrests, hospital stays, or rape kits.

Her drunkcapades could result in her bringing a strange man home, landing in the hospital after being hit by a car, passing out on the front lawn in freezing temperatures, sleeping in a drunk tank with a drunk and disorderly arrest, or filing a report at the police station after they found her raped and beaten.

This was my priming. This was the legacy my family left me.

I was determined not to be like my mother—sloppy, drunk and miserable.

While I watched her misuse alcohol starting in my early grade school years, I never heard the word "alcoholic" until I was in my teens.

I don't really know why the family waited so long to label my mom alcoholic. Maybe because no one thought she was alcoholic? There was a time when "alcoholic" meant people who could not conduct themselves with or without alcohol. Who, when they drank, were far removed from reality. Who, when they were sober, were so preoccupied with the need to get a drink they couldn't function. Mom would go weeks, sometimes months, without drinking.

Even with all her antics, today I see that alcohol was more like her vehicle to act brave and carefree, rather than a physiological craving. I believe if she had more confidence and guidance and felt supported, she wouldn't have needed the alcohol.

I learned early on that I had two very different mothers within one.

The first had a deep love for us kids. A mother's love. There is no denying it. No matter how reckless some of her decisions had been, she would let a lion claw the beating heart out of her chest to protect one of us kids.

She would drag herself and daughter miles through a blizzard to retrieve another daughter, if she had any

17

concern for her well-being. And she did.

She would take on bullies twice her size to protect her cubs. And she did. A high school girl came to our door looking to pick a fight with me. Mom gave my brother instructions to hold me in the house. This girl had my mom both in height and weight, but it didn't sway Mom any. She stood toe-to-toe with her and told her to get her ass off our property. Mom didn't budge when the girl swung at her. Nobody was touching one of her kids without killing her first.

My mom's love was desperate and absolute.

The second was afraid. It was as though fear had its own place in our family. If you took a family photo there it would be looming over my mother like an abusive spouse. I watched it rob her of living. When my mom didn't drink she was afraid.

Afraid something would happen to one of us kids, keeping us on a short leash.

Afraid Bob was going to leave her.

Afraid one of us kids was going to get sick.

Afraid of being judged.

Afraid of being stupid.

Afraid she wouldn't be able to provide for us.

Afraid about losing her looks.

She was afraid of everything.

Fear rose up in her disguised as anger and frustration. Instead of stating her needs or taking action to reduce the risk, she got mad. She either shut down and clenched her teeth or lashed out at my stepdad.

The only time she had a reprieve was when she drank. And then she drank as if to save her life. I can't imagine having that kind of paralyzing, all-consuming fear.

My heart hurts for her and all she missed out on.

When we got older and wanted to have sleepovers, she insisted on knowing where our friends lived. When she got drunk she would go to their homes. When they would ask her to leave (you always had to ask Judy to leave), she would start screaming, "You think you're better than me?" Her insecurities came out of hiding.

It typically ended in our friends being forbidden to be our friends anymore. So, we would ask, and then tell, mom to stop drinking. But it never worked.

Trying to tell her to quit drinking was like taking away her life pass. With alcohol she could talk to people, speak her mind, dance, live without worry, let go of her inhibitions, disconnect from fear. Without it she sat in the house, smoked cigarettes, drank coffee, cooked, and cleaned. Always watching the clock to retrieve us from school. Unless she kept us home where she knew where we were. That started in junior high.

No more drinking? That would mean no more courage to step out of the assumed identity of trapped mother, unfulfilled housewife and the plethora of names spewed at her by my stepdad. No more freedom to think about her own needs just for a moment. She knew she was a prisoner. Alcohol gave her the feeling she had some choice and some control.

My mom was just barely out of elementary school when she got pregnant with my brother. Mikey Flanders plied this fifteen-year-old girl with alcohol, knocked her up and off to the military he went. He was completely exonerated of any responsibility to her or his unborn child. She was discarded.

Her parents shipped her off to White Shield, the place you sent wayward pregnant teen moms back in the day. My grandfather didn't want my mom or the baby around the house. Mom told me with her lips pursed and gaze down while shaking her head, "I didn't stay. Two girls got in a fistfight and they were pregnant. I got my stuff, got on a bus, and I went home."

Back home, my grandma and her sister liked to drink at a Chinese restaurant down the street. That was where my mom would meet her keeper, Shaun, who owned the place. The grandparents were happy that Mom found a man to set her and baby up with an apartment of their own. They didn't mind that he was married.

My mother remained involved with her financier for about five years until she met my dad. The message, "Shaun was so good to your mom and Robby," still circulates amongst my family members.

"She was a looker," Dad told me when I probed him for answers thirty years later. He described how he stole my mom away from her married man, like a proud rooster. I guess Shaun didn't put up much of a fight for her, but with a wife, kids, and a couple successful Chinese restaurants at risk, that's no surprise.

One day my dad simply didn't come home from work, abandoning mom, my brother, myself, and his unborn child, Babe, formally named Sharina. Mom said she would get Robby off to school and then take me in the stroller to look for him.

This was perplexing to me. "What would you have done if you found him?" I asked her. She said she didn't know, but I did. She would have begged and pleaded, promised her soul, if he just wouldn't leave her.

After dad stepped out, one of the neighborhood boys, Bob, was happy to step in. Bob was a few years younger and had always been attracted to my mother. He slid into the caretaker position, and there he stayed through my childhood years. The years they served together were full of drama and damage. Mom wasn't happy, but whatever the welfare check couldn't provide, he did.

She got drunk, verbally assaulted him on a regular basis, and had many indiscretions. He volleyed back the verbal assault, walked out—sometimes for the night, sometimes for months—and on more than several occasions beat her bloody. I was maybe ten when he put her through the coffee table. When she stumbled to get up he doubled his fist and punched her in the mouth. That night earned Mom a new set of teeth. She wasn't thirty years old and had a top set of dentures.

Maybe there was a time when I was impacted by this, but at ten I just tried to distract my sister and moved us to another room. Hoping we wouldn't get hit.

"You're worthless," were his choice words for mom, and me as I grew older.

After fifteen years together, he walked out on mom, leaving her nothing.

A memory that will haunt me for the rest of my life (and I have many): Watching her crying and begging, holding on to his ankles as he dragged her out the door to start his new life with another woman. It still makes my heart constrict with pain. She was so helpless, hopeless and desperate.

I stood there in horror watching her plead, "Please, please don't leave me." Just, I mean, honestly, the desperation was palpable. I was afraid he was going to lose his temper and kick her away like an unwanted dog.

"Mom stop, please just stop." I cried.

I swore no man would EVER treat me like that. I would never be that weak. I would never beg for a man to stay.

Through the courts, she was awarded three hundred dollars a month for one year. Even I, an 18-year-old mother on welfare at the time, received more financial support. Mom came to live with me though I was barely able to care for my child and me. The drinking and drama didn't stop. Mom lived with me most years between 1986 and 2001, until I bought her a small manufactured home in an adult community.

She continued to drink, but I never had to retrieve her from the drunk tank or hospital, not for her drunkcapades anyway. Maybe because she had her own place and lived alone she wasn't trying to escape into the night. Staying home and drinking meant she didn't get into trouble. And, after the first few attempts, she didn't drunk-dial me anymore, because I'd just hang up. No fun in that.

Grandma Naomi

My maternal grandmother was a cantankerous broad. She chain-smoked with an ever-present Coke in hand, as she sat on a towel under the air conditioner, angry and bitter. She wore moo-moo type dresses hiked up and tucked between her legs, so as not to get any leaks on the dress. With one hand on hip and the other bent at elbow resting on the arm of the couch, she held her cigarette with the long thick fingernails at the end of her puffy fingers. Her eyes glazed with a slight film as she stared out the big picture window at the end of her sofa, bitching and gossiping on the phone.

I don't know anything about her childhood, though she didn't have an easy adult life. I know two of her daughters had different fathers. I also have no memories of her drinking. But there are plenty of stories in which she drank a lot and became angry and hostile without warning. My dad tells me that she drank big jugs of wine when she played cards with him once or twice.

Mom tells me she didn't like it when Grandma drank because "she got mean and would call your Grandpa names and Dad would, you know, hit her."

"One time Dad was so mad. He kept telling her to shut up, but mom wouldn't. So dad picked her up and threw her off the porch. Treece, (what she called me—short for Teresa) there had to be 8 maybe 10 steps," she said with a wince, like she was reliving it as she told the story. I swear in that moment I could see my mom as the little girl. "Mom was mean when she drank," she said, looking down at her feet.

Grandma Fern

My father abandoned us when I was just two or three years old. Both my paternal grandparents had died before I was even born. I established a relationship with my dad in my thirties and we connect every now and again. When I have questions, he answers them to the best of his ability.

I feel there is bitterness in his heart for both his

parents. He gets real descriptive and seeks out the right words for most memories, but when it comes to his mom, Fern, he's very short and almost dismissive. He talks about his dad's gambling and how he left him with his stepmom, Sharon. I don't think he's aware of the change in his demeanor when he speaks of them.

"She was a Honky Tonk woman."

This didn't sound so bad to me, but there was clear disdain in his voice. I looked up the definition: *"A woman with no particular skill who entertains cowboys in the saloons or dance halls."*

His mom left him and his two sisters when he was three years old, just like I was when he left. I see the pattern but he doesn't connect the dots. He resents his mother for the very act he repeated and seems quite unaffected by.

Fern died in October 1953. As Dad tells it, "She was killed by a drunk driver. She was the driver."

She was driving a Buick between taverns on the main road to Mt. Rainier, between Elby and Ashford, Washington. Dad said she made a bet with someone that she could drive from Ashford to Elby, have a drink and return to Ashford in a set time. There were three guys in the car with Fern—not one of them was her then-husband.

The road curved slightly in a small, block-long town called National. She misjudged the curve and ran head on into the church, knocking it off its foundation. Fern was the only one to die in that accident. The guy riding shotgun had a broken leg. She was about 33.

They have since moved the church. Dad was just ten years old when his mom died. His father took Dad and his two sisters to see the car not long after the accident. Dad revealed no emotion as he told me the engine was in the back seat. That's his survival mechanism – detachment. If he doesn't feel anything at all he won't feel the pain.

But me, I feel something when I think about her. I'm sad I didn't get to meet the woman who thumbed her nose at societal pressure to be proper and do the "right" thing. Abandoning your children is never okay. But a woman hanging out in bars and racing cars in the '50s? That took some nerve. She had moxie.

The world viewed her as a Honky Tonk woman... I

can only imagine the pain of that—and of being so disconnected you'd leave your children. And what was it like for her to discover during World War II that she had been born to German parents before being adopted in the U.S.?

What else had happened in her life? I wonder.

Alcohol is the obvious tie between all three women.

But they also made a lot of poor choices. The kind of choices that can cause emotional, if not spiritual, pain. Choices that would be hard to reconcile within the soul. And those unreconciled choices only festered and caused more pain, leading to more poor choices.

And the cycle kept repeating.

The more women like this are badgered and condemned for their behavior, the more pain they feel and the greater their need to medicate.

You might think the obvious—that I was doomed to be an alcoholic because addiction is genetic.

In fact, genes have very little to do with addiction, says Dr. Lance Dodes, an addiction specialist at Harvard Medical School and Massachusetts General, among other institutions.

Dodes writes: "A summary of research over the past 35 years shows that for alcoholism, by far the most studied addiction, there is no genetic factor for most people. There is a subset of people who may have increased genetic risk but we now know conclusively that there is no single gene for alcoholism."[2]

When I started exploring the legacy I'd been left by the women before me it wasn't to confirm that I was alcoholic. I wanted to learn more about their lives in order to understand why they drank.

And what I found was pain. Different levels and different kinds. But pain nonetheless.

The women weren't passing down a gene as much as they were passing down misinformation about how to live abusive and ignorant lives. How to not use their voices and own their power. How to feel helpless, hopeless and in pain—and not be able to change.

According to Dodes, addictive-type behavior restores a sense of power to the individual who at some point

---

[2] http://www.lancedodes.com/frequently-asked-questions/

feels overwhelmed with feelings of anger, guilt and shame[3].

I can see this in all three women, can't you?

I don't believe alcohol was the problem for the women in my family. I believe pain was.

I've been working with women for years and while some of us have extreme stories and others don't, the pain is the same.

Don't underestimate your pain by comparing your experience to someone else's.

If it takes space in your psyche—it matters.

It takes a lot of energy to live with dissonance--telling yourself that something doesn't matter and pushing down the true feelings that are begging you to set them free.

As women, we often mistake being cold, heartless and disconnected as being strong. I want to offer you another perspective on strength. Being strong is facing, feeling and walking through the storm and deciding it will not break you.

---

[3] http://www.lancedodes.com/what-is-addiction/

I was primed. I learned from my ancestors to suffer through and settle for whatever was dealt to me—that I have no control to change it. And I learned that alcohol does a pretty good job of soothing the pain caused by all that suffering and settling.

I've learned that living like this is not living—it is a slow painful death. More than thirteen years ago, I nearly died settling for the mess of a life I had created by numbing the pain and not believing I could change.

In the following pages I will share with you in rapid succession my journey.

"The measure of a woman's character is not what she gets from her ancestors, but what she leaves her descendants." — Unknown.

CHAPTER TWO

Disconnecting

There is an old Native American parable that says there is a battle between two wolves within each of us.

One wolf is love, hope, grace, compassion, patience, peace, confidence.

The other wolf is anger, doubt, fear, envy, guilt, jealousy, shame.

They battle to be fed and dominate the soul.

Which one will win?

Depends on which one you feed.

My Aunt Ruthie was my connection to God.

She was a church-going, non-leg shaving, dress-wearing, judgment-doling, mean ole broad, who had a laugh as jolly and a belly as big as Santa Claus.

She was the matriarch of our family and ruled with a booming voice and heavy hand.

And every Sunday morning and evening and Wednesday evenings she joined her brothers and sisters for worship and service. Here she raised her voice and her hands to the heavens as she cried and sang.

The Bell Rose Pentecostal Church of God was her church home and the closest thing I had to my own. I can still smell her cheap, obnoxious perfume and hear her sing, "There will be peace in the valley."

Every few years she grew restless and abandoned the church and all her values. She'd smoke, curse, wear pants, watch R-rated movies, and tell dirty jokes.

But eventually she always returned home to Belle Rose.

I'd like to say that going to church and not drinking

cooled her anger and improved her behavior. It didn't. She was abusive by today's standards. Not just to her kids, but also she dominated (more like, emasculated) her husband.

I remember a drunken scene with Aunt Ruthie. The kitchen was dimly lit by the light from the dining room. There was a whiskey bottle and terrible yelling. Uncle Windy was holding his hand up to his head, covering his ear. There was blood oozing through his fingers. My cousins and I were hiding around the corner in the room next to the dining room. Trying not to look, but trying to understand what was happening. And that's it. I want to say she broke the whiskey bottle over his head, but I am not certain of that. I was no more than four or five years old.

Though my mom could be aggressive in her drunken state, I remember watching Aunt Ruthie beat my mother down, giving her a large black eye that stayed put for weeks. Mom had shown up drunk and started attacking Aunt Ruthie's husband, Windy. "You're fucking worthless like the rest of them. Yah, you sit there with that smirk." As Mom took a swing at him, BOOM! Down went Mom. All of us kids were scared and started crying as we were running up the stairs to the bedrooms.

Like my mom, Ruthie was also a fierce protector. She questioned Mom and Bob when they dropped me off for the night, with welts and bruises on my little legs. Mom kind of shushed her: "I know… He got carried away. It won't happen again."

Bob once found me taking the clothes off my life-sized doll and kissing her. He took the black cord that went from the coffee pot to the outlet and said, "You are a bad girl. Don't you ever do that again. Don't ever do that to your doll." He swung and swung again. The cord wrapped around my leg and when he pulled it back, it would grab the welt already there. The pain was awful.

This was not completely abnormal back in those days. Many of us would have been in foster care for the beatings we got. Aunt Ruthie wasn't much better and she didn't reserve her spankings for just her children. If we stayed overnight without Mom we were susceptible. But if Mom was there, it was rare she'd let Ruthie hit us. "Tend to your own kids. I'll tend to mine." Mom was so much stronger than she thought.

This Little Light of Mine

I am grateful for Aunt Ruthie because she was my connection to God, church, and Jesus. She brought us to church mostly for Sunday school, Easter, and Christmas Eve service. I liked the Bible stories in the bible and loved the songs we'd sing. "This little light of mine, I'm gonna let it shine" was one of my all-time favorites. Still is.

I enjoyed getting away from home. The Sunday school teacher was a great storyteller and used a felt board with characters to act out the scenes. It was always great fun to play with new kids and listen to them when the teacher would ask what we thought about each story. It felt safe and joyful in Sunday School. I believed I had a special friendship with Jesus. I kept that secret, though. I just thought I knew Him differently or maybe it was He knew me differently than they knew me. Jesus knew my secrets.

When I started understanding the adult messages, however, religion was lost to me. At the Sunday and Wednesday evenings, things got scary. The preacher stood up at the pulpit and with that same booming voice my aunt used for intimidation, told us how vengeful, angry, and unforgiving God was. He'd yell so hard sweat poured off him.

Instead of comfort and joy at church, the messages changed to lakes of fire and God's disappointment in me, how I was a lowly sinner and would be judged, and how I could never measure up to God's expectations.

As I grew older I recognized hypocrisy far and wide in the church. Like how Ruthie turned on again and off again—I'm Ruth the church lady, I'm Ruthie the rebel. It was confusing. While the church people would say to love one another, they'd whisper and gossip about each other. "Can you believe she would wear that to church? I heard she had an affair. She's living in sin with a man and not married."

Love one another… but if someone didn't fit the ideal of their perfect churchgoer they wouldn't love them. At least, it didn't feel like love.

I felt if I could never please God and I was doomed for damnation, what the hell was I doing then?

I disconnected to find peace, or maybe it was to not

feel the weight of my damned soul, believing I'd never be accepted by God. I simply stopped talking to or thinking about God. I acted as if, there was no such thing.

What nobody knew was I was already damned.

My body had been sexually used most of my childhood from my earliest memory by a family member. Soon it would be my brother's friends. They would sneak into my room and mess around with me while I was sleeping—touching my private parts and touching themselves.

When I would wake up and realize they were fondling me, I was too afraid to say anything. Afraid of what? I'm not sure. Making them angry, embarrassing them, getting them in trouble, embarrassing myself, getting myself in trouble? So, I would lie there pretending I was still asleep. Hoping they would stop. It wasn't so many years since I'd gotten whipped with a coffee cord for undressing my doll. I didn't want another whipping.

Why do they get think they can touch me like that? Do they talk about it with each other? Why is this happening?

There was one particular friend of my brother's. He was seventeen and I was twelve. I stuffed my tube top with toilet paper and put beans in the middle as makeshift nipples to attract his attention. He was the local equivalent to Scott Baio (don't laugh—he was hot back in the day.) He wore real cutoff jeans that frayed on the ends, tank tops and long, striped tube socks. His brown, feathered hair fell over his light eyes. I would lay out in the sun in our front lawn and watch him and his friends skateboard the halfpipe they built in his driveway. I loved him. I wanted to believe he loved me. I even broke up with a really sweet and cute boyfriend who I really liked for him. Serious stuff for a twelve-year-old girl. He worked at a burger joint and smelled like he dipped himself in grease and he had bad acne. I remember always wanting to pop the big gross whiteheads so I wouldn't have to look at them any longer. Couldn't HE see them?

But he was so hot and he was seventeen. He had the coolest hotrod although it didn't run much. He liked me and I felt special. He would come over pretending to see my brother so my mom wouldn't freak out. Having been the young victim of a seventeen-year-old boy herself, she didn't want me repeating her mistake.

One-night mom had a hangover and fell asleep early. We usually just snuck kisses and touched each other's private parts when she left the room. But since she was passed out we snuck off into my room. I loved him and wanted to give him whatever he wanted. It felt good to have him want me so bad. He pulled down my underwear and crawled in between my legs. He put his thingy in. It hurt, but it didn't matter because I knew he was mine now. I knew he loved me.

We heard mom coughing and thought she was waking up. He jumped off me and pulled up his pants.

When I whispered, "That was really good, huh?" he said, "It doesn't really count because we didn't go all the way."

What did he mean it didn't count?

"I didn't finish. I didn't cum. So it doesn't count," he whispered. My ruptured hymen told it differently whether he came or not.

When boys messed around with me sexually before,

I didn't think God would be mad at me. I didn't want it done to me and I didn't like it. But now that I wanted a boy to have sex with me and let him have sex with me, even though he didn't cum, I was damned. There was no returning from my sinful ways. Filled with sinful thoughts about boys, my body had become a weapon against my soul.

I was going to hell.

Damned If I Do…

My final connection with God and religion was pleasant. But it made me come to a harsh realization. When I was 12, my girlfriend, Gina, invited me to her Baptist church's summer camp. She was such a sweet girl and her proper mother was quite a contrast to mine. Their simple apartment was quiet and serene. It was the summer Anne Murray's song, "You Needed Me," played on the radio. I'd sing along. She sang about how she sold her soul and he bought it back for her. How she needed him and he was there.

Of course, I wouldn't know the real meaning of those words until nearly thirty years later. I want to say that camp stirred up the same hate, fear and condemnation I felt at Aunt Ruthie's church. It didn't. It was one of the best memories of my childhood.

The camp sat up in the mountains. We swam in the huge pool at least twice a day and sunbathed in the warm sun. We made "graveyard" drinks that were a mix of all the sodas. Each room held four girls and a counselor and we'd laugh and tell stories until late at night.

My counselor really liked me. She talked with me about how I was enjoying camp and said she liked my bathing suit. She made me feel like I mattered. Shannon was one of my cabin mates. She was cute, silly and quick-witted. We became like best friends over that week trying to out-tell stories to each other with exaggerated details. I felt like a kid. I was surrounded by these great girls and engaged in all the activities. In truth, I don't remember anything churchy about the camp. Not a single sermon or prayer.

What stood out to me, though, was my self-condemnation. I wasn't like these girls. I was damaged and broken and if they knew the truth about me, they wouldn't have liked me. I could forget during the day when we were busy and doing things, but at night my secrets would haunt me. I knew the truth of who I was and by the time we were ready to go home, I was resolved to quit pretending.

I Would Never Be A Good Girl

Rather than trying to become what I could never be, I disconnected from God and the good girls, to be on my own. Gina and I were very different girls anyway. We just never talked again. I stopped thinking about God. I did the same thing I did with Gina. I walked away and never looked back.

I was twelve.

Coincidently that same year I experienced my first intentional drunk. Doug, the next-door neighbor, would sit out on the front porch and talk with us kids. He eventually invited us to follow him in to the house and get comfortable in his home. Then it became natural for me to just pop in and chat. Mom was so glad I had him to talk to, because I didn't get along with my stepdad and I'd never met my real dad. What my mother didn't know was that Doug was plying me with Rainier beer, while kissing and fondling me inappropriately.

I liked how beer allowed me to disconnect from my feelings. And while Doug was kind of old and gross, his touches and kisses weren't awful. Not like when I was a little girl—I hated being touched when I was little. For once, it "felt" good not to feel bad about being bad.

My momentum picked up from there. In eighth grade I drank as often as I could, smoked pot when I couldn't drink, started smoking cigarettes and got good at having sex.

That year, I reconnected to the boy I loved since kindergarten, Ricky. He had big, brown eyes and long lashes; dark wavy hair and a wide, sweet and mischievous smile I couldn't resist. His Cuban family didn't subscribe to traditional methods of parental supervision, so he was able to run amok. No curfew. No one following him around, like my mom did with me. No rules or discipline.

Which meant every time I skipped school or lied to my mom and didn't come home, I was with him. That's the only way I could be with him. My family were bigots and refused to accept or permit me to date a Cuban. My stepdad was the worst: "Cubans are just one degree from being a fucking nigger." I know…it's awful.

I didn't care what anyone thought. I was in love.

During one of these unsupervised rendezvous, I had sex with my new love. And I got pregnant. I thought I just had a stomachache—I was so confused. I don't remember a conversation or making the decision to have an abortion, but my stepdad and mom drove me to the Kaiser hospital on Greeley Avenue in 1980, and my brother's girlfriend's mom picked me and mom up. I was so detached through the entire process. Dropped off, shown into a small room, told to put my feet in stirrups…On the way home we stopped at Taco Bell.

We never talked about it again. We never did, but I heard whispers at a family reunion at Blue Lake Park that summer.

"Did you hear? Teresa found herself in trouble."

Trouble was code for pregnant. Now everybody knew what I knew all along. If I hadn't already been certified as broken and condemned before, I most certainly was then.

Through my teen years I drank with Ricky and his

friends. I went to house parties and drank when he and I were broken up. Pretty typical, I'd say, for a teenager who was primed to party and had murdered her conscience. Pretty typical for a teenager who had disconnected from God and herself with no moral compass.

Ricky's older brother changed during the years we were together. He used to go out to the bars a lot and keep several girlfriends. Each thinking they were his main squeeze. But now he was skinny and hid in his house a lot. I found out he was using cocaine. This was a major, big-time drug.

Ricky and his best friend Tom came over to my mom's house to pick me up. "Let's go in your old room," Ricky looked wild eyed and moved his head in that direction. He pulled a tiny white envelope from his pocket. Tom had a small compact mirror and razor blade in his hand. When I looked up and caught Tom's eyes, I knew something was up. His eyes were wide and he didn't seem to be blinking.

Ricky dumped some white powder on the mirror and divided it into three equally matched lines. He rolled a dollar bill and stuck it up one nostril, plugged the other and snorted the powder right up. Ricky handed it to me. "Oh, come on, babe, you'll love it. There's nothing like it."

I took the dollar bill and snorted my first line of coke. I liked it. I liked it a lot. For this 16-year-old, nothing felt better than a few lines and a couple cans of Hamm's.

When I got pregnant again not long after this, I quit using and drinking. But my Cuban love did not. He continued using and began freebasing cocaine during my pregnancy. I'm pretty sure it's called smoking crack these days.

It's funny how memories from long ago still live within your body and cause the same anxiety as they did so many years ago. Just thinking about this makes me feel anxious.

Freebasing is what Ricky's brother was doing and it changed him from a charismatic Cuban gigolo into a skinny, paranoid weirdo. I was scared. What was going to happen to my Ricky?

The night and dark morning hours before my precious baby arrived, I'd been up begging his dad to stop using: "What if he comes tomorrow? We have nothing. No diapers. No formula. Nothing!"

Ricky relented just before dawn and finally we went home. After the sun began to rise and I had convinced him there was nobody on the roof, he fell asleep. I don't know if I'd even dozed when I flung off the sheets to see that I had wet the bed. My water broke. Ricky rushed me to the hospital and slept in the waiting room while I was terrified and in tremendous pain giving birth to our son, Cody.

My maternal sobriety didn't last long. About two weeks after I brought my baby boy home, I joined his father in the chase of my life: freebasing.

The want that directly followed each hit was maddening. After spending all the money, we had, begged or borrowed, lips stuck to the glass pipe all hours of the dark, I'd lie there and beg the demon to stop calling me as I tried to sleep away the craving for more.

Our son couldn't have been more than six to eight weeks old when I gave his dad an ultimatum: Stop the drugs or I'm taking our son and leaving. I only used when he used and if he didn't use, I wouldn't use. I don't know what motivated me more—that we didn't have money to pay bills or that he was taking off to party with his friends. But he made his choice and so did I.

I took Cody and moved back to my mom and stepdad's. I was scared and uncertain how I was going to raise a child on my own, but I was more afraid of what would happen if I stayed. I'd watched Ricky's family members shrink in their lives and, as it turned out, I hadn't seen anything yet.

I never did crack cocaine again. That doesn't make me innocent and I was no hero. Because it didn't take long for me to be smitten with a brand new infatuation—crank. You know it as meth. Hello, lover! This was the greatest drug ever invented. I didn't have to spend as much money and could stay up for days. It would only take a dime, ten dollars, to set me up for a full night and early morning spin. I could drink all night and not get drunk. I lost weight. A girl's dream diet.

Living with my mom and stepdad meant I had a built in babysitter. I would head out on Friday night and not return until Sunday.

I wanted more of staying up all night and started hanging out at a friend's house playing cribbage for hours on end, smoking, snorting, and drinking. In this small shack that was unheated and falling apart, people came and went at all hours. One night, my friend's cousin Mark walked in. Tall, handsome, intense—and recently released from prison, he had a no-nonsense confidence that pulled me like a magnet.

Mark and his whole family, as it turned out, were not only dealers, but they were manufacturers of crank. I graduated from the "bad boy" I was typically attracted to; this guy was dangerous.

We had only been dating a few weeks when we pulled up to Mark's cousin's house and she met us outside, "Teresa, your mom's trying to get a hold of you. Your little boy has a fever."

I was high-strung, and hospitalized with random fits of vomiting and not eating being identified as "stress related," in my teen years. Being high on meth made it even worse.

Cody had had spinal meningitis when he was two or three months old. I almost lost my little man then. Because of that any fever would cause me great concern. That night, at ten months, he had a fever and couldn't keep his food down. Mom rode with us to the emergency room. I felt like I was coming unhinged, but I didn't tell anybody that.

I will lose my mind if anything happens to my Cody.

After a careful examination the doctor assured me it was nothing to worry about. They prescribed him some antibiotics and sent us home.

On our drive back to mom's house an emergency vehicle passed us, lights flashing and siren blaring. My body froze, my eyesight went blank. I felt needles pushing from the inside of my body out. I couldn't catch my breath. I could hear my mom as if a mile away, frantic, "What's wrong with her? Please, what's wrong with her? Mark, help her!"

It was my first massive panic attack.

About a week later, we woke up to a bright and sunny June morning. I instinctively connected the panic attack to the crank and didn't want to trigger another one, so I was clean and had my bearings.

Mark ordered me to make breakfast. When I said no, he pulled me by the back of the hair, bringing my face nose to nose with his. "Get your ass in there and fix me something to eat, you little bitch or I'll kick your fucking ass."

Feeling secure thanks to my overprotective fierce mother in the next room, I yanked my hair out of his hand. "Get the fuck out!" I yelled. He left. I never heard from Mark again.

That was the end of my dope days.

Unfortunately, it wasn't the end of my panic attacks.

And it wasn't the end of my disconnection.

When I was young and happily listening to Bible stories in Sunday school, I didn't realize that I was already damned to hell. By now, I'd connected the dots from my sins to God's anger and vengeance.

I understood perfectly that I was alone.

I disconnected from God, my spirit, and my conscience when I realized I was too bad to be saved and, like the women before me, chose to feed the hungriest wolf.

"One is evil — he is anger, fear, envy, guilt, shame, resentment, lies, self-doubt.

CHAPTER THREE

Defeated

No matter how bad things are you can always make them worse.

--*Randy Pausch*

Cody, me, and my mom makes three...for most of the next sixteen years. During a short stint where it was just Cody and me, we moved to a small one-bedroom apartment where my sister, Sharina, lived just a few buildings down.

This is where I met Rex. A cocky son of a bitch with the then-fashionable permed mullet hair, he stood six feet and three inches tall. He had a slight but muscular build, big blue eyes and a dashing smile. When he'd come cruising through the parking lot with music blaring, I'd run to the window to catch a glimpse of him. He knew I liked him. I could tell he was not into me. His apartment was conveniently located between mine and my sister's, so I would walk by a hundred times a week, hoping for a hello.

Rent was tough to cover with my welfare check, but I was finally awarded Section 8, low-income housing, which would make life much easier for us financially. I found an approved property in the next county over. It was a clean and spacious two-bedroom duplex just outside city limits.

It wasn't until I moved out of the apartments that Rex and I started fooling around. I don't know what precipitated him to acknowledge me then. Maybe it was easier to hide the fact that he was going out with me. I can't even say we dated. No movies. No dinners out. Our six months together consisted of drinks and lots of sex. It's embarrassing, but true—I was his booty call.

In late winter 1988, I invited him to a paid-for beach weekend with some friends of mine. After I repeatedly kicked his ass at cards and backgammon and teased him about it, he threw a drink in my face, grabbed his stuff and stormed out. He was going to leave me there. The only people left were my sister and her friend who drove up in a two-seated Fiero, with a gear-shift between them.

How the hell was I going to get home? I did what I had to do. I chased after him and begged, "Please, give me a ride home. You don't have to talk to me or ever see me again. I just need a ride home."

Rex drove a small brown low-rider truck that wasn't a comfortable ride to begin with. His coldness made it even worse.

He took me home and that would be the last I saw Rex for a while. I later found out he started seeing someone else.

The summer of 1988 marked a big shift for me.

We were living comfortably, my welfare check covering the rent. Mom had been living with Aunt Patty for a couple months until she was evicted for her drunkenness and bad attitude. When Mom wasn't drinking she had this shitty edge about her—making snide comments and rude remarks with an air of entitlement.

"I wouldn't have no man sitting around not working," she'd say, referring to my aunt's husband who graciously allowed her to stay in their home. I felt I had to take mom in when she burned out her welcome at Patty's… and my sister's… and my cousin's.

We'd have a two-week window of peace and gratitude before I could feel her discontentment build.

When she exhaled with a disgusted and dismissive grunt I knew she was not pleased with me. It could be something as small as me talking to a guy on the phone or even leaving for work. She was just miserable.

When I started working, it made me crazy when she snarled and turned her back to me. Working was a privilege for me, but she made it seem like I was going out partying and leaving her home with the kid.

Like a spoiled little girl pouting because she couldn't have her way: "I never get to do what I want." She never used those specific words, but her actions screamed them.

A child I could ignore or deal with, but a grown adult I was helping out? It was maddening.

I knew something was going to blow. And it always did. Driven to ease her suffering she would take the grocery money or kids' piggy bank money, excuse herself from her duties and get drunk.

When my sister and I were little girls, my mother's behavior scared us because of its randomness and rage and the inevitable abandonment. She always fled, perhaps in search of the life she was too afraid to live sober.

As we turned into teens we saw her behavior as our opportunity to run amok. Now, as adults with children of our own, it was terrifying…and embarrassing. When you asked Judy to babysit, you couldn't count on her not to get drunk and abandon your children. She would usually notify someone that she was leaving, but that didn't mean they would watch your kids.

When Mom moved back in, I got a job and then two and, eventually, three. I was hooked on working and being productive. I loved the feeling of working in exchange for money and had a deep desire to be independent from all assistance.

Do you know what that meant to a girl like me? My mom never worked. She was never independent. I was going to be different. Yes, I was going to give Cody opportunities I never had. Cody was going to experience life with a parent who could provide for him and never abandon him. Encourage him to dream big, go after life and support him in his interests. He would feel loved and cared for and have higher expectations for himself.

I took public transportation to downtown Portland. First stop, Goose Hollow. I arrived in the early morning to clean rooms in the college dorms. At noon I would catch a bus up to the Nautilus health club where I worked the front desk, and then head back downtown to Payline Systems to process long distance calls all evening.

"Hello, this is your Payline operator, how would you like to place your call?"

They were kind to me and wouldn't make me work past 10:30pm, since the last bus out to the then rural Clackamas County left at 11:30pm. I walked half a mile in blackness from 82nd Avenue to our home. I was fueled by a deep desire to break the cycle. I was willing to do whatever it took NOT to be angry, bitter, drunk, and dependent like my mom.

With a boost to my income, I bought new clothes, added highlights to my dark ash blond hair, and started tanning. I felt like I transformed from the ugly duckling to a swan that summer. And it's true about confidence being a girl's best accessory. I didn't lack in attention from guys.

I drank occasionally— when I went to the nightclubs with friends. But with my work schedule, it wasn't often. I don't know how I fit it in but I was seeing a few different guys at this time. I'd receive roses at Nautilus from one guy and another would show up to take me to my next job and be upset about having to transport the bouquet.

To my friends' and family's dismay, one of my suitors

was Rex. Yes, the guy who was going to leave me at the beach and used me as a booty call. He was the one I wanted. Today, I know it was about proving my worthiness. He didn't want me, so if I could get him to want me, *then* I would be worthy.

By Christmas 1988, we were more or less living together, and by spring I was pregnant. I have to be honest that while I thought, "He is mine now," I didn't get pregnant on purpose. I couldn't take the pill because it caused visual disturbances. At first the doc called them mini-strokes, but later diagnosed them as auras connected to migraines. Whatever they were, they would terrify me and then trigger panic attacks.

I don't know why I thought having his baby would keep us together.

It didn't work for me and Cody's dad.

It didn't work for my mom.

Rex looked good on paper. He was attractive, had his own apartment and a job, his own car, and was going to school for electrical engineering. I felt like I had hit the jackpot. I was worthy. I had someone who had everything going for them and who wanted me—

somebody who was heading in the right direction.

We got married.

Upon our return from our honeymoon, his mother and father came for a visit. They sat at our kitchen table and handed us a large manila envelope stuffed with all his bills: car payment, insurance, school, and a various few others. I felt like I had gotten sucker-punched. I can't remember if it was before or after this that he quit his job.

Everything I had believed was untrue. His parents were taking care of his bills. What looked good on paper went up in smoke. He struggled to keep a job because of his entitlement and temper. Now he lived with me and I took care of the rent, utilities and food. He dropped out of school and the student loan came due for repayment immediately.

I was angry. Hurt. Betrayed. And trapped.

I was now providing for all of us. And several months pregnant.

I didn't want to believe my fairytale was going tits up.

I started working for a brand-new company earning a significantly larger salary. But since they had just opened their doors, medical insurance wouldn't be available until March. I worked right up to delivery. At my Valentine's Day checkup, the doctor said, "Baby is doing fine. He's about six pounds, and I'll see you next week."

We got home, I stretched out on the couch and, swoosh, my water broke. I didn't get anxious and hysterical this time. I knew the drill. When I told Rex my water broke and lifted up the blanket, he asked, "Is there supposed to be blood? "

"Well, there could be a little," I responded. I pulled off the blanket and saw blood everywhere. I wanted to scream, but didn't. The blood ran down my pant legs and puddled on the couch cushion underneath me. It kept gushing out. I had to sit on a blanket riding to the hospital to absorb the flow.

Instinctively, I stayed calm for Cody. It had been snowing for a couple hours and the roads were in pretty bad shape—especially, the long, steep winding road up to OHSU, where I was expected to deliver. We opted for the closest hospital, Providence Milwaukie, and I was checked in at 7:30 pm.

They wheeled me into an exam room. The baby's

heartbeat was weak, the umbilical cord was wrapped around his neck and I was losing a lot of blood. They decided on an emergency Caesarian. As I lay there listening to my heartbeat on the monitor, looking at the bright lights above, someone told me to start counting backwards from 10. "10, 9..." Austin arrived healthy with no complications at 7:41pm.

He was perfection—skin flushed and healthy looking. A crown of golden curls that sparkled under the lights and a full, round face. Nearly three pounds bigger than expected, he looked older than a newborn. My Austin was here.

My restless baby slept very little and we'd try everything to comfort him. We sat him on top of the washer in his carrier hoping the motion would lull him to sleep. We put him in an electric swing and drove him in the car. He just preferred to be awake —a lot.

But we were all excited with the new addition to our family and Cody was a fantastic big brother.

My maternity leave had been approved for six to eight weeks, but I was the only one working and we needed money. I tried to go back to work in a week, but I was still bleeding and weak from the surgery. I went home for another ten days.

Austin was a blessing, but the unexpected surgery and stay in the hospital would eventually bankrupt us. Rex didn't work full time, when he did work, and I didn't make enough to pay for it.

Thus began my abusive reign over my marriage. I was angry. I assumed the persona of my aunt Ruthie: I ruled with a booming voice and a fuck-you attitude, and didn't care one bit about emasculating my husband. At the time I was proud of being a bitch and not taking any shit. I wasn't my mother.

On Friday nights I would knock a few back with the people from the office and come home late. I felt a kindred spirit with my Grandpa Bud who often opted for a night of drinking and stumbling in whenever. This probably contributed a great deal to my Grandma Naomi's bitchiness.

Our roles were definitely reversed. I was not kind to Rex. When I had found out he had been reconnecting with his ex-girlfriend, the rage burned me from within, and I clocked him with the bedside phone. It's not funny and it's awful, but it's the truth. I held him in great contempt. How dare he see her while I was working and providing for our family?

I had constantly worried about his ability to remain faithful. As it turns out, I had good reason.

The day they came to repossess my car I had had enough. I resented that I worked so hard to establish my independence, only to be forced into bankruptcy because my husband threw temper tantrums and walked out on work.

The boys and I got a place of our own and Rex moved into an apartment a few blocks down the street. We played nice for a quite a while. Rex was the only dad Cody had known while his dad, Ricky, was sick with crack cocaine. Cody called Rex "Dad" and Rex stepped into the father role. That was an admirable quality I couldn't deny.

When we moved into our own place I started learning a lot about me as an individual. A woman. I started running regularly three to six miles as often as possible. I loved to run. Who knew? I would drive from the office across town to Lake Oswego and pick up the boys after work. We'd head back over to Gold's gym in NW Portland, where I would meet with friends to take a step class or lift. The boys really enjoyed the playroom there.

For the first time, I was really taking care of me, not just surviving. I listened to new music—country, funk, and smooth jazz. The smooth jazz was amazing and could transport me to a place of sensuality and sophistication. I still appreciate it today. I started drinking wine instead of beer, but drinking was not the highlight of my life. I loved being active.

It was a good time for me. I was promoted from Marketing Assistant to Sales. I was experimenting with lifestyle preferences. I was growing. I was independent, again.

While Rex I weren't divorced we were living separately and getting along. Feeling like I was moving forward again in my life gave me a fresh perspective and we decided to give our marriage another go. It was short-lived. I could not trust Rex.

The breaking point was the day I learned he was issued a driving citation in my car while I was out of town. This may not sound like a problem, but Rex was uninsured and had promised he wouldn't drive my car. I just couldn't trust him to be truthful about anything and his acts of defiance jeopardized what I thought we were working to put back together after the bankruptcy. This broke what was already fractured in our relationship. It was over.

I started communicating with my former mentor and boss, Tory, who had moved down south. He was handsome and sharp and I trusted him implicitly. At our old company, he'd helped me improve in the workplace and gave me many opportunities to advance with guidance and advice.

This made a huge difference in my confidence and abilities as a professional woman. I started as a long-distance operator in the call center, and was promoted to receptionist and then human resources assistant. My skills advanced with each promotion— from problem solving to computer skills, which were just becoming a hot commodity. I learned to, as he once suggested, "Take the bull by the horns, show initiative." When that company fell on hard times, I was able to leave with my pick of better paying jobs and more opportunities to grow my skills.

I crushed on him badly while we worked together, but we were both married and I never acted on it. I never even spoke of it. I suspected he was attracted to me too, but never said anything--it was just a feeling.

Tory was coming to town for a contract and asked if we could get together. I was delighted. I still mattered to him. This man I'd put on a pedestal wanted to see me. He cared. He was still married, so I told myself our reconnecting was innocent.

We started with dinner and then, on his next visit, we watched "Wolf" with Michelle Pfeiffer and Jack Nicholson. It was summer 1994. He started joining me at parties and dinner with friends. We'd always had fabulous drinking times together. Back in the day, I was known to perform a few dances on the table, tell dirty jokes, talk like a foul-mouthed sailor and use the men's room to pee when the ladies line was too long. He appreciated my "don't give a damn" attitude and I think my willingness to be taught also appealed to him. When he gave me advice, I'd run with it. I was willing to work for success and I was committed to achieving it.

Within a few more trips to Portland for work, it happened. My wildest fantasy had come true. The man of my dreams wanted me, too. Tory—the older, successful, handsome, educated and brilliant man wanted me! Well, at least when his contract would call him away from his wife and children. He would make my travel arrangements and I would meet him wherever he wanted.

It was fun. I had the love of a "good man" who showered me in gifts, including a flip phone so I would never have to miss his call. Though we kept our relationship from the boys for quite some time, they eventually called him "Uncle Tory."

My mom had remarried during this time to a man neither Sharina nor I were a fan of. But that wasn't the worst of it. During their marriage she was diagnosed with and beat lung cancer. What we didn't know was she was suffering through domestic abuse. When we'd visit mom during this time she would cry uncontrollably.

"I don't know why I'm crying," she would sob. We thought it was menopause. Now I'm not so sure.

Late one night I received a call from the police department. Mom was in the hospital. Her husband had been arrested and charged with abuse and kidnapping after tying her up in the back of his van and torturing her periodically. She managed to escape and someone called the cops. I picked her up and brought her home. The next morning, I took her to the Clackamas County Courthouse to file a restraining order and she came to live with us again. She wasn't drinking while she was married to this guy. Perhaps she felt she needed to be sober to survive.

With mom at the house again it made my rendezvous with the married man easier.

"Tory's really good to you and the boys," she would say.

Talk about an eerie coincidence. Reminded me of when the family used to talk about mom's married man: "Shaun was so good to your mom and Robby." Of course, I didn't tie the similarities together.

The novelty wore away and the pain of being the other woman became hard to live with. He lied like so many do. I'd give him a deadline and, when it came, I would break up with him. We played this game for six years.

It didn't take long before the weight of being his whore eroded my confidence and self-respect. Each time I went back to him my self-worth died a little bit more and the need to ease my pain with alcohol grew at a rapid pace. As an account executive, I had some freedom in my work schedule. Being out in the field calling on new and existing customers allowed me to sleep off my hangovers. But I was losing my edge. Once known as "tenacious" and brought in by senior execs to disarm the difficult customers, now I would barely pull myself together to troubleshoot client issues, and not much more than that. Forget about cold calling and new client development. Eventually, I quit before I was fired and moved around within the industry for another year or so.

You've Been Served

It was getting dark. To get to my front door you had to open an iron gate and walk through my private courtyard. It was concerning to see a strange man approaching my door. "Are you Teresa?", he asked. "Yes." I responded. "These are for you," handing me an envelope. He was a process server.

Rex did the inconceivable: he filed for divorce and requested full custody of our son—along with some other outrageous demands. He was living with his parents and I knew this wasn't his doing, but his mother's. It didn't make sense. We were getting along fine.

I called him crying and in hysterics, "Why are you doing this?"

"I didn't know. I'll take care of it," He sounded honestly surprised.

We agreed to find a fair and neutral attorney. Because he was first to file, it gave him an advantage and because he worked very little during our marriage compared with me, the borderline workaholic, he was the primary parent to our son. No argument there. We would maintain joint custody with Rex being the primary parent. Austin would live primarily with Rex and I would pay child support, but we would make parenting decisions together.

As the divorce proceedings were going on, Rex still continued to pick up Cody, who continued to call him "Dad."

One day, Rex picked Cody up, took him to his new girlfriend, Myra's, house where he and Austin now lived. He kept Cody in the truck for several minutes while he went inside. When he came out, he drove Cody to my sister's, and dropped him off. Cody was not allowed at Myra's.

Cody was upset, asking "Why didn't I get to go to Dad's?" and "Does this mean Dad isn't my dad anymore?"

I didn't ever really answer Cody's questions. I couldn't. I didn't have the answers. I was gob-smacked. This was a devastating blow to our peaceful co-parenting relationship. I hated him for his cruelty to Cody. It was unforgivable. Rex never spoke to Cody again.

It only got worse. Rex and Myra decided I no longer needed to see Austin and wrote a scathing letter to me about being an unfit mother. It took me six months to get in front of the judge, but that letter sealed the deal finding him in contempt of our agreement. I wish I could say that was the only time I would be in court enforcing my right as a mother. I would go through hell and back with my ex for the next few years just to exercise the visitation rights that had been decided by the courts. Just to be in my son's life.

The game of keeping my son away from me didn't end until I filed asking for primary custody to be turned over. The judge ruled Austin would continue living with Rex, but assured Rex if she saw him in court again (meaning, if he kept my son away from me one more time) he would go to jail.

Even with that promise, I felt defeated.

A Change of Scenery

My impressive resume still got me jobs pretty easily, including an account manager role with a technical recruiting firm in Seattle. This was cutting-edge back in 1997. And after losing my court battle, I needed a break. A new landscape and something promising to focus on. I never missed a visitation. Upon accepting the position, I negotiated to leave early every other Friday.

During the day, I enjoyed my team of co-workers and my clients. The challenge of learning a new city and a new industry thrilled me. But the nights and weekends I wasn't in Portland seemed empty. On weekends, Cody and I would explore the area, and then I would settle in with my companion, booze. I didn't want anyone to get close and find out how much I drank or discover my involvement with Tory.

So much shame. The loneliness and pain being away

from my friends and family intensified.

I transferred to the Portland office and moved back eight months later. But the problem drinking and poor decision making wasn't ebbing. If anything it increased. Again, I quit before they fired me.

I was completely detached from the girl I used to know. I got a job at a smaller company with less opportunity. I didn't pursue anything better because what if Tory wanted me to fly away or finally left his wife? I started smoking again and put on fifty pounds of shame and guilt.

I was turning into a washed-up drunk.

I was broken.

I needed and wanted help. But when I went looking the only option was Alcoholics Anonymous. I wasn't an alcoholic. I just wanted to slow down. I wanted to get control over my life again.

March 2000

My electricity was disconnected for nonpayment. I'd pawned all the jewelry Tory had given me to put food on the table and beer in the refrigerator. I was drinking a six pack at least twice a week and getting wasted on the weekend.

I blamed him. I blamed him for my being broke and unable to care for myself and my kids. I blamed him for who I had become. I told myself I was waiting for him to move forward with us. But the truth was, I lost hope in myself. He promised he would come to my door someday and be free. That day never came.

I'd like to say after I dumped the married man, I regained my composure and stepped back into my once driven self.

But I didn't. I was wounded and left without any spark or energy. I was so far back from where I had started, I couldn't see how to move forward. I even considered saying "Fuck it," and going back to public assistance.

I had tried so hard not to be like my mother, drinking too much and dependent on a man and there I was. I didn't behave as badly, but the end result was still the same.

I thought my mother's personality was the reason for her drinking problem. I didn't get drunk and rage like she did, so I had nothing to be concerned with. I certainly wasn't alcoholic. I wasn't like her.

But that one poor choice of getting involved with a married man, then going against my values and dumbing down my conscience with alcohol left me susceptible to making another poor choice and another.

I had become my mother.

"Addictive tendencies arise in the parts of our brains governing some of our most basic and life-sustaining needs and functions: incentive and motivation, physical and emotional pain relief, the regulation of stress, and the capacity to feel and receive love…" [4]

—Dr. Gabor Mate, In the Realm of Hungry Ghosts

---

[4] http://drgabormate.com/book/in-the-realm-of-hungry-ghosts/

CHAPTER FOUR

Darkness

"When someone shows you who they are, believe them the first time."

— Maya Angelou

"One who deceives will always find those who allow themselves to be deceived."

Niccolo Machiavelli

What was left of me was indiscernible. The thought that I once was somebody or at least *could be* somebody had crumbled. This belief could lead to nothing good.

September 2000. I tipped my toes into online dating. Back then we had match.com and excite personals. It was pretty exciting and a softer way for this girl who was having a hard time with identity to do her best to put the pieces of her life together again.

It had been six months since I told Tory goodbye and I didn't want to fall back in the cycle of calling him. I had lost my confidence and felt vulnerable. I wanted someone to love me. I went on a couple different walking dates. For me, it easier to get to know someone when we weren't stuck sitting in a coffee shop or restaurant just staring at each other. They were nice guys, but it never went past the walks.

Until Prince Harming answered my ad. He was funny and seemed self-assured, definitely a charmer. He said all the right things: "I don't settle. I go after what I want. I thought I wanted to be a country singer, so I took off to Nashville for a couple years and partied with Waylon Jennings, and wrote some songs. It's a tough scene to break into."

I liked his big picture dreams and that he had guts to go after them. I needed someone who could inspire me to do that.

When I showed my co-worker Penny his picture, she said it looked like he was wearing prison blues. Red-faced and unsure of what she meant (but could conclude), I questioned him later. He told me he had his own business, lived in the affluent neighborhood of Lake Oswego, drove a Corvette (a car I've always had an aversion to) and bred mastiffs. He never mentioned prison. Penny had to be wrong. He assured me it wasn't a prison uniform.

In the picture, he also wore sunglasses and a big grin. I mentioned how important a beautiful smile was to me and he told me about how important dental hygiene was to him. He said his mom had spent thousands of dollars on braces to give him a great smile—and that he always chews gum or sucks on mints. I remember thinking that was odd. What did gum or mints have to do with hygiene? I wondered. I let it go.

Gals, pay attention to those little nudges.

I asked if he had ever been married or had kids. No

and no, he answered. I was a bit surprised that a man in his early thirties hadn't done either, but maybe he was wiser than most. Maybe he was saving himself for someone special. Maybe I was "the one."

Come on, we all have fantasies.

Then we met in person.

Our first date was a walk along the Willamette River. On my way to meet Prince Harming, I was heading west on Harold Street and a car came out from nowhere, crossed my path and stalled in the middle of the road, blocking my passage. The thought actually occurred to me: "Turn around! Don't meet this man." Like I was being warned. But when the car moved aside, I shook it off and continued on. Upon first impression, I was confused and amazed. So much for the beautiful smile. He had one capped front tooth that was considerably larger and whiter than the other and the rest of his teeth looked damaged. They were dingy, mercury filled and not much in alignment. If mom spent thousands, there was no sign of that investment.

But he explained it away, "I got in a motorcycle

accident. It knocked out my front tooth and the cap was supposed to be temporary. Hey, I got busy and it just hasn't been taken care of yet." I, being vulnerable and damaged, accepted the explanation. I was amazed that our pictures of dental hygiene and a beautiful smile could be so opposite. And amazed at how someone could be audacious enough to plant such a big, misleading expectation. It was baffling.

Perhaps that was part of his witchcraft. Disarm with audacity.

It worked.

He was driving a Corvette, older and not well kept, but a Corvette. There was a mastiff, Rasputin, sitting in the front seat. So some truths offset the...misleading information about the smile, *(Today I'd call it a lie)*. I have to admit he was funny and told great stories. His plan, if he had a plan, worked. I agreed to keep talking with him and see where it went.

Soon he was sending flowers to my work. It was nice to have the attention of an available man. We were having some fun. He seemed open about his life and who he was, told great stories of racing muscle cars at the professional tracks and meeting some of the greats, like John Force, the NHRA top fuel drag racer. He told me he was Italian and alluded to mob ties, "If we (his family) had a problem with you, we take care of the problem."

He had lived in Vegas, was raised in California and hadn't met his father until recently. That's what brought him to Oregon.

He invited me over to meet his dad and dad's girlfriend.

The address was technically in Lake Oswego, but a part I had never visited. This beat-up old house was filthy from top to bottom. Dirt, slobber and the mud produced from the two combined coated everything I could see. What furniture there was, a random chair and a make shift table, had visible dirt and mud all over it. It looked like they did most of their living in their bedrooms and the rest of the house was mastiff domain. Several beastly mastiffs had the run of the place.

I had assumed that, being a business owner and living in Lake Oswego, he was a home-owner, but this was a rental. My assumption, my bad. And he was not even the tenant. The house was actually rented by dad and girlfriend, so Prince Harming was a guest.

The "business" turned out to be a commercial newspaper route and I would call it more of a contract, than a business. Besides, it was his dad's contract, not his. Now, most people would cut and run at this point, but no, not I.

My reasoning: He didn't lie outright and my sister had recently suggested that maybe my standards were too high. And honestly, honestly, I couldn't imagine anybody lying to such extremes. Surely, it was me--I had made the wrong assumptions. Not his fault. Prince Harming was very attentive, doting, and, I have to stress, charming. Everything a broken-hearted gal with a shattered identity needed to feel a little bit better about the world she lived in.

If there had been any window for me to come to my senses and withdraw from this cunning man's grasp, it was quickly closing. The company I worked for shut down their offices and downsized to remote workers. I was let go. I received a small severance package and qualified for unemployment benefits, but this felt like the final blow to my ego and any sense of who I thought I was.

What I was, was terrified.

This couldn't have been a better scenario for Prince Harming.

"I have these skills and this trade and with the small investment from your severance, we can make things happen. *I will take care of you*," he said.

At this, every last one of my defenses dropped. I was overwhelmed and felt powerless. I needed someone to take care of me.

He got to work and lined up a contact at Fleetwood Manufactured Homes. He knew how to finish up a manufactured home and make it ready for the owner after delivery. He knew all the intricacies of repairs for these types of homes. Although I didn't know this trade even existed, it was in demand at the time. Manufactured homes were being repossessed in large numbers and banks were paying contractors to make them retail-ready.

He packed up my Honda Accord with what tools I had, as he didn't have anything, and headed to Washington to do a job and demonstrate his skill. It worked. He had forged, fronting as an established contractor and business, his way into securing contracts with Fleetwood.

His dad was getting angry that Prince Harming was no longer available for the night deliveries. He and his girlfriend left messages like this on my voicemail: "If we don't hear back from you, we are going to tell your pretty little girlfriend everything."

I swallowed hard and asked, "What's going on?" A part of me wanted to believe nothing was wrong. He assured me they were crazy and angry and making up stories. Once again, I chose to ignore the warnings.

Because of the rift between him and his dad, I agreed he could stay with us. Oh, God, I know. It's horrifying the danger I exposed not only myself to, but my boys. As it turned out, Austin loved him, and Cody accepted him. In a matter of a couple months from initial meeting, I had a construction business with this man at the helm and I was buying a manufactured home for us all to move into.

During this whirlwind, I learned he was indeed an ex-con and still on parole. That's why he was staying with his dad. He'd moved to Oregon for a fresh start. The night he finally admitted it he wouldn't let me out of the car and insisted he couldn't live without me. He kept running red lights to keep the car moving. Eventually he made me promise not to jump out if he pulled over. It never occurred to me to lie. I promised.

He begged and pleaded, "I was at the wrong place at the wrong time. It wasn't my jacket I was wearing that had the drugs in it. My attorney was totally paid off and I took the fall. Come on, baby. We are building something here. Look we've started a business--it's all in your name. You're set. I'll take care of everything." He wore me down.

To my injured soul these words were quite intoxicating. He needed me. People can change. Maybe it would be my fairytale and we would live happily ever after. He had never had someone like me before. Plus, I was fucking exhausted. I relented.

Prince Harming loved being the center of attention and the hero. He plied Austin with attention and treats and tried to connect with Cody, but they couldn't relate with each other. Easygoing Cody stayed in his room and started gaming. I think Prince Harming's big personality sometimes overwhelmed

Cody.

I insisted on doing business legitimately. I got our federal tax identification number, I took and passed the general contractors exam for the state of Oregon, I set up all the business bank accounts. Becoming a general contractor opened up a wide arena of work and we started bringing in subcontractors to help knock out more jobs. The business grew rapidly.

The boys and I had never experienced so much expendable income. We hosted big barbeques and karaoke parties. You never had to worry about bringing your own beer, when you came over. I bought a top- of- the- line treadmill, hoping to get inspired to run again. Cody got a car for Christmas one year. We outfitted the whole house with new furnishings. There was a lot of money, and we spent it as fast as it came in.

Soon not letting me out of the car progressed to grabbing me roughly, restraining me, and frequently bending my fingers or hands so far back I cried in terror, "It's going to snap!" The pain was excruciating, but the fear was paralyzing. He called me names, "You're a fucking bitch. A goddamn gold digger. A lazy motherfucker."

My drinking increased to daily. I was my own boss and didn't have the distraction of a schedule or supervisor to keep me from numbing out and hanging over. My drinking didn't bother him. In fact, he encouraged it. He bought a beer refrigerator that he kept stocked. "Need another one?" he always asked.

Sleeping with the Devil

One day there was a knock on the door. A gentleman asked my name and handed me an envelope, "I'm a process server. You've been served."

I opened the envelope and read that Prince Harming was being court ordered to pay child support for not one but two children.

He denied knowing anything about these children. The mother was a jealous ex-girlfriend who had cheated on him and blah, blah, blah. One night in a moment of consciousness, I ordered a background check and the list of marriage certificates and aliases that came up was mind-numbing. When I confronted him, he threw a lamp at me and it shattered against the wall. The more he raged the more I drank. More, faster. That night when he climbed on top of me to have sex, I swear I saw the devil. His face contorted as my surroundings were melting and the ceiling was pulling away. I felt like I had sold my soul.

He insisted he wasn't the father and would take blood tests to prove it. He created a big story, "The lady knew me when I was in Nashville and was just trying to attach herself to me because I was on the road to becoming famous. I'd only met her a couple of times and she needed a place to stay."

"Why did you tell me that she was a jealous ex-girlfriend?" I screamed.

"I don't know, I'm scared. Just don't do this. Don't end what we have." He would exhaust me with contradictions trying to keep the stories straight.

I believe he believed he could will what he wanted. That he could manipulate every situation.

Of course, the children were his and the mother…was his wife…still. They lived in Salem, where they all had lived together at one time. Why did I stay? It was complicated.

Not only did I rely on the business to give me and my kids what we needed, but he was also a master in breaking me down and believing I couldn't get by without him. It sounds cliché, but I truly believed that nobody else would ever want me.

Look what I had become.

I embodied worthlessness.

Prior to Prince Harming, I would have never expected I could be a victim of domestic abuse. At the age of eighteen--I told the Meth man, Mark, to get the fuck out when he pulled me by the back of my hair.

I had sworn no man was ever going to have that kind of hold on me.

One night it finally happened.

Prince Harming beat me. He punched me in the head and face repeatedly. I thought I was going to die. I begged and pleaded not to take me away from my sons. "Please spare me!"

I don't know if it was to take a breath or get his footing, but when he stopped for a moment I made a dash for the front window and crawled out. I stood screaming in the middle of the road, "Help! Call the police!" No one offered to help. No one called the police. He was on parole and he would have been taken away. It would have ended right there. We lived in a manufactured home community with neighbors less than fifteen feet away on either side. Why did no one call? I will never know.

Prince Harming stayed at my aunt's place for a few days, calling me relentlessly. He was a conman; he knew how to get what he wanted. He knew how to build support from my family and have them speak for him. It didn't hurt that they worked for us and were paid well. They had a vested interest to keep us together.

My bruises healed, I grew tired, and I got drunk. He came back.

Of course, he promised to quit drinking and never to hit me again.

His tongue dripped lies as if part of his DNA. At first I couldn't comprehend that someone could lie like he did. So, instead of listening to that little voice of inner-wisdom that was telling me: "His story's not lining up," I silenced it with alcohol.

I was deeply entwined with this man who was violently abusive. He could be set off by very little and was capable of a lot. We argued constantly and if I were an ignorant woman I might say, "I can understand why he pummeled my face. I deserved it."

Buying the Farm

He stopped drinking for a while and we got busier than ever with the construction business. We had opened one office and then another because of storage constraints and soon bought and moved into a hundred-year-old farmhouse. It offered a large garage space where we could centralize all the tools, materials and company vehicles to save on overhead.

The farmhouse looked beautiful. The past owners did a great job of planting beautiful flowers around the front of the house and added a rich red cedar siding that gave it tremendous charm. It looked picture perfect.

The boys got to choose what color they'd like to paint their rooms. Cody chose a rich red and Austin a soothing blue. Cody's room had a slider out to a deck and was the only bedroom on the first floor. At seventeen this gave him a feeling of being grown.

Austin's room had a huge picture window that looked out the front of the house and was filled with light during the day. They were both excited that we were buying our first home and had a great big yard for dogs and barbeques. The boys loved the parties.

More court orders arrived. One revealed that he was married to yet another woman. Yes, he had two other wives at the same time, not including me. We were never married.

There is nothing I could say to make you understand how I still stayed with him after learning this, unless you have been in a similar situation.

My life was so ensnarled with him as the puppeteer, I had no hope of ever being free -- emotionally, physically, financially. He worked wonders with creditors and opened lines of credit in my name that I never had to sign for. As I watched in disbelief, he convinced a US Bank agent to approve me for a ten thousand dollar line of credit right over the phone. She asked for me to get on the line and give her permission to talk to him, but that was it. The control he had simply by being audacious, patient, and arrogant blew my mind.

One sunny afternoon we were driving to bid on a job when I spied a very ordinary scene. A woman and child laughed and played in a small, overgrown yard. The plain house could have used some maintenance. But they looked so happy. They looked free. I envied that woman and couldn't forget her.

How could I have so much, money and furniture and things, and be absolutely miserable-- while they could have so very little and be so happy?

I wanted simple and nothing.

Something was shifting.

Still I began most mornings asking the same question, "Why am I still here?"

I would roll over and reluctantly open my eyes. I don't know how long I had been asking this question, but it was part of my morning ritual. I wasn't suicidal and never considered taking my own life. But I was tired, so very tired. I had no interest in living, and nothing, not even my kids, inspired me to get up and start the day. I looked forward to nothing except the moment I could numb the dull constant pain that had become my life.

I had never known pain like this--waking up each day and knowing that my life was under the rule of a man and there was nothing or no one that could save me.

One poor choice after another after another had turned my life into a living nightmare and I was being buried alive.

One night between Christmas and New Year's 2002.

The karaoke machine was going. We had a houseful of guests. They were singing, drinking and doing what we had always done, partying. But I seemed to be in another world.

I remember the fading sound of music as I schlepped up the narrow dark stairs. I felt like I was having an out of body experience. Part of me was awake and aware while the other was drunk and weaving.

I stumbled across the top floor hall where the old oak tree swayed on the other side of the windowpanes and threw menacing shadows on the wall. Was I dreaming?

The music echoed through the old farm house, like in a movie when someone is on a bad drug trip and the music seems separate from reality and off in the distance.

Heading into the bathroom, I got undressed and slid into the shower.

Does anyone know where I am or what I'm doing? I thought to myself.

Why was I taking a shower? It was like I had this independent consciousness coexisting with drunkenness.

And in what seemed like slow motion my arm and hand twisted around the shower curtain, my feet lost connection from the shower floor and the shower curtain came down, rod and all on top of me. I lay there for a moment, blinking my eyes trying to catch up to what just happened. I stumbled to my feet, turned off the water, and rehung the shower curtain and rod. Other than being a little stunned by the fall, I was okay.

I felt trapped somewhere in my mind. I had a sudden realization that my body was not under my control, but in the control of the drunkard. But my mind was awake. It was kind of scary.

Then I threw up. In all those years of drinking so

much, I'd never thrown up. Well, maybe once when my teenage girlfriends and I shared a gallon of vodka between three of us. Not getting sick was a curse and a blessing. It didn't matter how bad my stomach would hurt, I wouldn't be able to vomit and get relief. But I was never the girl that got so drunk she threw up.

I was a clear mind trapped in a drunk body, which terrified me. Yet what happened next scared me even more.

I brushed my teeth, combed my hair, got dressed, and numbly followed the old hallway, crept down the narrow staircase, and made my way across the dining room. I walked through the kitchen and into the beer cavern, our back porch with the refrigerator reserved for beer.

I proceeded to open a beer and drink it.

I felt like my soul surrendered that night. It made a plea. It fought to get my attention and I swallowed it down with a cold Michelob Light.

Could you imagine feeling like even your soul is giving up?

Eerily enough, I don't remember anything after that. Maybe when my soul relented it returned my mind to the state of the body.

Drunk.

I became acutely aware of the empty darkness within me.

No light.

No hope.

No soul.

"No amount of sleep will give you rest if it's your soul that's tired."

"Not every story has a happy ending, ... but the discoveries of science, the teachings of the heart, and the revelations of the soul all assure us that no human being is ever beyond redemption. The possibility of renewal exists so long as life exists. How to support that possibility in others and in ourselves is the ultimate question."[5]

— Gabor Maté, In the Realm of Hungry Ghosts: Close Encounters with Addiction

---

[5] http://drgabormate.com/preview/in-the-realm-of-hungry-ghosts-introduction/

PART TWO

FOG

Faith is taking the first step, even when you don't see the whole staircase. Martin Luther King, Jr

Now faith is confidence in what we hope for and assurance about what we do not see.

Hebrews 11:1

CHAPTER FIVE

Doctor

When the student is ready the teacher will appear.

I wake up. My heart is racing and my mind is reeling. Something's terribly wrong.

In recent months, I wake up between 2:00 and 4:00 every morning with an overwhelming feeling of doom. My body is tight in anticipation of an unforeseen danger. I'm holding my breath.

Breathe. I must keep breathing. Where's a paper bag? I think, hoping to avoid hyperventilating, which will inevitably be followed by a full-blown panic attack.

I crawl out of bed and tiptoe downstairs to the living area. The house is dark. It's just me and my thoughts. Not a pleasant place to be.

Am I going to have a heart attack? A stroke? Maybe this is a sixth sense and something terrible is about to happen.

I sit down.

No, can't sit.

And I pace.

Something is wrong, but I can't identify exactly what it is. My mouth is dry. I go for water. It didn't matter how much or how late I drank the night before, I could no longer stay asleep through the night. Alcohol had always been my go-to for sleep. It shut down my brain that raced through endless avenues of the coulda-shoulda-and-what-ifs. It occurred to me to fetch the tequila in the cupboard above the sink. I never cared for hard liquor, but I knew if I took a couple shots I could melt back into oblivion. I couldn't bring myself to cross that threshold. If the regular routine and volume of drinking didn't qualify me as having a problem, using alcohol to get back to sleep in the middle of the night certainly would.

A few months back, I had seen a mental health specialist for what I called my night terrors. I never thought my drinking was connected to them. I just figured I was just losing my mind or was, according to the buzzword of the times, "depressed."

It was quite a process just to be seen and be heard by a mental health professional.

First, I had to request the appointment through my primary care physician.

My primary care physician had to recommend me for an interview for the mental health department, with an understanding I was in danger of harming myself.

I then had a phone interview with a mental health department staff member and they determined if I would be seen.

I was coached by my primary to say I had thoughts of harming myself to expedite the process and secure the appointment.

This was a lot of hoops to jump through for help. Especially, for someone "in danger of harming themselves."

I'd thought a lot about death, but never about hurting myself. I suppose that's just semantics when you consider my abusive behavior with alcohol and my relationship with Prince Harming. I got the appointment.

I hoped to get some answers, help, anything that would give me some peace.

I checked in at the front desk. I kept my eyes low feeling a mix of embarrassment and shame. I was sure to mind my own business and make no eye contact with anyone.

"Teresa?" A couldn't-be-more average man stood

there in khaki trousers and a white button-down shirt. Brown, thin hair with a thin mustache and beard to match. He wore glasses and an expressionless face. I followed him to his office. He motioned me to a chair that sat on the side of his with a good space between the two. I waited for instruction. He seemed nice. Calm. Something I wasn't accustomed to these days.

"Why are you here to see me?" he asked.

"I wake up in the middle of the night almost every night in terror. I can't get away from the feeling or reason it away. It persists for at least an hour, maybe more, before I can get back to sleep. I feel like I'm losing my mind."

Until that moment I didn't really think I was depressed. I didn't know what I was. But right then, I felt hopelessness invade my being. I don't know if I brought it with me or if the act of seeing a mental health professional unleashed it. But I felt the darkness closing in on me.

"Do you drink?"

I was completely honest: "At least six to eight beers most nights and about fifteen to twenty when friends come over a few times a week."

"What about blacking out? Any memory lapses?"

"I rarely black out. I do have a struggle trying to reconstruct the night before at times."

I hated that. Especially, if I'd done or said something hurtful to someone I cared about. Like yelling at Cody for something stupid like not taking out the trash. Or the worst, making promises to the boys: "We'll go to the movies tomorrow. It'll just be us." And forgetting the whole conversation only to meet their disappointed faces the next day with, "I'm sorry, I forgot. We'll do it another time." That was painful.

"I can't get to sleep without drinking."

He didn't miss a beat, "What's your stress level like?"

Huh, he didn't even blink an eye about my drinking. Maybe it wasn't such a big deal?

"I have a good amount of stress. I own and operate a construction company." *Among many other things*…I thought to myself.

There was a brief pause. And he moved on, "Great weather we're having," while he scribbled on his pad, nodded, and glanced at me a couple times. Letting out an exaggerated breath, he said "Well, here ya go." He had no expression, but if I had to name one, it would be bored.

Looking back, I'm surprised he didn't ask questions like: Do you feel safe? Is your boyfriend hurting you? Have you thought about not drinking?

Our time was up. He handed me two prescriptions. Oxazepam to treat anxiety and Prozac for depression. Hopeful that doc knew best, I went straight to the pharmacy and filled the prescriptions. I had been prescribed anti-anxiety meds before. In 1987, I called the paramedics thinking I was going to die; they concluded it was the Xanax that triggered a panic attack. I had tried anti-depressants before, but hadn't really given them a chance before dumping them.

Perhaps these were the magic pills that would make everything all better.

On the ride home it was real quiet, but that didn't last long. Prince Harming started in with questions about the medications they prescribed. "So, what'd they give you?"

"Something to help with anxiety and depression."

"Oh yeah? What're the names?"

"I don't know. I don't think they're narcotics. I told him I drank a lot."

"How do you know?" he asked. "Have you ever taken narcotics? Do you even know what narcotics are?"

"Well, no," I said. "But why would they prescribe me narcotics to get high when I'm already drinking a lot?"

"Just give them to me." He grabbed them from me, glanced at the labels casually and tossed them back over.

Somehow I knew where his interest in the meds was going: A different kind of party in a different kind of bottle. But I had never been interested in pills. My grandma Naomi had a big bright yellow sewing box full of meds. It sat across the room next to the television, filled with brown prescription bottles with white caps varying in size. There wasn't room for a spool of thread or a thimble. I dreaded getting old and having the same fate. I didn't want to take a pill to live. Let alone a box full.

I read through the side effects and warnings. I

thought it was odd that doc would prescribe me a medication that could be addictive. Red flags went up. I didn't want to have an addiction to pills. I went on to read "Do not mix with alcohol" on both prescriptions. Well, there went the magic solution. I decided to hide the bottles in a safe place for someday—maybe someday. It never occurred to me to take them while drinking and not drinking was out of the question.

This Doctor Was Different…

The day after New Year's 2003, I woke up a little fuzzy from drinking the night before. Lying on the bed I noticed something was off with my vision. I couldn't see what I looked at directly. Then the prisms started. Dancing lines of color and light, like when you hold a crystal or diamond up to a light at just the right angle. It started in a tiny spot and spread over a larger part of my vision. My brain raced to mini-stroke, auras, migraine. I had experienced these before. But only when I was on birth control pills.

After all those mornings I questioned why I was still here, I now wanted to stay. My boys were heavy on my heart and mind. I couldn't leave them.

I was scared. I needed help. I needed to go to the emergency room.

I woke Prince Harming to tell him I needed him to drive me to the hospital. He got out of bed and started stumbling around. Oh, gawd, he was still drunk.

It was cold and grey out. Drizzling. A typical Pacific Northwest wintery day. As he drove, I wondered:

Am I overreacting? Is he still too drunk to drive from last night? What if something is really wrong with me? What if nothing is wrong with me?

No answers to any of these questions followed. I sat there like an obedient child waiting…for something. Waiting for my head to explode, my heart to stop, to have an uncontrollable urge to open the car door and jump while driving 60 mph down the highway.

Something was changing in me. I hadn't been able to experience any relief from alcohol in weeks, maybe months. I had a feeling of emptiness and was unable to escape in my usual way through the booze. I actually felt like I couldn't get drunk enough to escape my reality.

The other night when I schlepped up the stairs and slid into the shower while the party was happening downstairs, did my soul make itself known then because I was getting ready to die? Or maybe it was fighting for me to live?

My mind seemed to be processing a hundred miles per minute. Not sticking to anything. More and more questions rolled in. Still no answers.

We arrived at Kaiser Sunnyside hospital. It was early in the morning so just a few people were waiting to be seen. Good. I was sure it was all for nothing. My vision had cleared by this time, since the auras typically last thirty minutes from start to finish. The eyesight cleared but there is always remnants of exhaustion and jumpiness that lasts for hours. I was there and I still didn't know what triggered it since I was not on the pill. I figured I might as well stay and be seen. Prince Harming was propped up against the wall in the corner across from me.

Man, he's gross. I turned away as if he was a figment of my imagination and hoped he would disappear.

"Teresa Martin," a nurse called. She had me step

onto the scale. What??? 218lbs. What the hell's happened to me? I followed the nurse down the hall to an open door and walked in, Prince Harming was in tow. She took my vitals and told me the doctor would be in in just a moment.

I let out a held breath.

The door opened and in walked this kid. He must have been mid-twenties, maybe thirty. He had bright eyes, a light beard with a head of curls, and pleasant demeanor. "Hello, I'm Dr. Warren."

I was immediately disarmed of any fear that I was overreacting or being silly. He had a vibe of helpfulness.

He went over the standard questions you might expect from a general practitioner in an emergency room. "How long have you been having these? When did they start? Have you had them before?" And then he asked me, "Do you drink?" I answered honestly, the same as I had before.

This time, THIS doctor, was different. He shared with me about how women's bodies; organs and brains, start to break down much faster than men's do from high levels of alcohol consumption. He asked me what my origin was, I told him, "Irish, German, I know for sure and a little Pennsylvania Dutch, I think."

I threw in, "A mutt in general."

He smiled. "Your Irish heritage may be in your favor in regards to physiological damage. I'm going to order a round-up of blood tests. We'll check your liver enzymes and a few other things."

"Now, about the panic attacks…." he went on. He grabbed a tongue depressor and bent it back as far as he could.

"When you drink at night you're suppressing your anxiety, but when the alcohol wears off in the middle of the night, it's like a spring board." Here he released the tongue depressor and it snapped up and across the room. "When this happens it shoots you from one to a hundred instantly. That's why the sudden terror. If you want to get a hold of your panic and anxiety, quit medicating with alcohol."

Medicating with alcohol? Am I medicating with alcohol?

This grabbed my attention. I would have never figured my drinking as medicating. But it made sense.

Dr. Warren was cool. He scribbled lab orders on his clipboard and then looked up at me with what I can best describe as a thoughtful expression. He didn't smile or look overly intense. But there was kindness his eyes. I remember that well.

"Have you ever considered getting help with your drinking?" he asked.

"I have no idea. I don't even know where to begin."

"We have an outpatient program here at Kaiser. Give them a call and look into it. It's a good place to start."

Dr. Warren wasn't overly sweet. He didn't tell me everything was going to be okay. He did tune in to me. He was present and talked with me almost like maybe he could relate or had a special interest in alcohol and the effects on the body. He took time to ask me questions and told me how I was damaging my body. He educated me and gave me helpful information. He handed me the brochure to follow up on the outpatient program.

I felt like I had a choice for the first time in many years.

Prince Harming was in the exam room with me the whole time. If he wasn't, I think I would have told the doctor everything. I would have told him about the abusive relationship, if he would have asked. I can't help but think he would have if Prince Harming wasn't there. I liked how Dr. Warren paid zero attention to my affliction sitting in the corner.

I was nervous about the tests they took to check for damage to my organs. Dr. Warren seemed concerned with how long I'd been drinking and the amount of alcohol I consumed.

What will I do if they say I have irreparable damage? What if it is too late? Oh my gosh, I weigh 218 lbs. It stops right here, right now.

Because Prince Harming had served time and was on parole for the conviction of: felony for distribution of a controlled substance, he was court ordered to attend AA and NA meetings. He was well versed in the ideals and talk tracks of alcoholism. He began his preaching immediately:

"Alcoholism is an incurable disease. Believe Dat," he would end every statement like it was gospel. Never mind that he drank, as much and frequently as I did.

And who said I was an alcoholic? I guess it was assumed, since I wanted to get help with my drinking.

When we got home my boys were still asleep. Prince Harming went back to bed.

I started pacing and wondering if I should follow through and call for more information about outpatient treatment.

I felt a little excitement. What if I stopped drinking? And then I felt a little fear. What if I stopped drinking! There were so many pros and cons.

Then I stopped thinking and just picked up the phone and dialed the number on the paperwork Dr. Warren handed me.

A woman answered. I blurted out, "Hi, I need help," my emotions collided over the internal struggle and as if hit by a tsunami of tears, I started crying. I felt a release. Almost like I had some power restored just by making that call. Hope was found in that small decision. Maybe this isn't all there is. Maybe I still have life to live.

It was done. I was scheduled for my intake with Scott, at the same mental health offices as before.

Oh, the thoughts that were flooding my mind.

Can I do this? How can I live without ever drinking again? What's that even look like?

I made a decision to stop thinking about it and wait to see what this program was all about.

Prince Harming kept telling me that I was going to have withdrawals because I drank so much for so long. He went on to tell me about worst-case scenarios, including seizures, vomiting and diarrhea. "Believe Dat."

Oh great, I'm waiting for my lab results and may already be dying from liver failure, now I'm going to have seizures and shit myself?

He also frequently reminded me, "Relapse is part of recovery. It's expected that you will drink again."

I decided, that's not going to happen…at least not until I find out the results of those damn blood tests. I could feel my resolve slipping. But I would not let it go until I met with Scott.

Please, let Scott say something, anything, to help me.

CHAPTER SIX

Outpatient

"Being ignorant is not so much a shame as being unwilling to learn." — Benjamin Franklin

"People use drugs, legal and illegal, because their lives are intolerably painful or dull. They hate their work and find no rest in their leisure. They are estranged from their families and their neighbors. It should tell us something that in healthy societies drug use is celebrative, convivial, and occasional, whereas among us it is lonely, shameful, and addictive. We need drugs, apparently, because we have lost each other."

— Wendell Berry, The Art of the Commonplace: The Agrarian Essays

It's intake day! I was nervous and a little excited. I had not had a drop of alcohol since my visit to the emergency room less than a week before. It had been good because I hadn't had any detoxing with seizures or diarrhea. My night terrors ceased. I received all my lab results back and I was not going to die from liver failure. Yea! Shockingly enough, through all Prince Harming's prepping, my not drinking was going differently than he had planned. I had no withdrawal symptoms nor jonesed for a drink.

I was counting my blessings, literally spoke my gratitude daily. It kept me from chasing the booze rabbit down the hole to Drunkville. Reminding myself that I had been given a reprieve with no damage to my body renewed my resolve to not drink. Prince Harming was taking me to my meeting with Scott. Nothing new there. He insisted on going with me.

Please don't be allowed in the meeting, I pleaded inside my head.

"Teresa!" Scott peeked his head around from behind the door.

"Yes," I answered while standing up.

Prince Harming started to stand, "You can go ahead

and stay seated. We'll be about 45 minutes or so." Scott stopped him.

I exhaled and smiled just a little on the inside.

My leash has some slack. *Wow, there's a leash!*

Prince Harming waited for me in the waiting room. Of course, he didn't need any help. It was me with the problem. My resentment against him was building. I hate how he schools me about how I'm going to be or what I'm going to experience. Fuck him.

I noticed immediately the similarities between Scott and the last guy I met with about my night terrors. Was there a mental health field "type?" Scott was about 5'9", slender build, brown thinnish hair, no body or wave, parted to the side and swept back. He wore a short beard and round-lensed glasses. Other than being a bit older he could have been the same guy.

"So, tell me what's going on," Scott prompted.

I shared with him my history with alcohol and about my recent interlude with Dr. Warren. I mentioned alcohol had always been a part of my life and can't imagine life without it. His lips were pursed together,

"Uh-huh" while nodding his head.

"I think you're a great candidate for our program" he said. "It's twelve weeks long. Looks like your insurance provides full coverage. It's me and another facilitator, Veronica. Both of us have had our own experience with recovery. Yah, you can get started next week." He pushed some papers back on his desk and turned his chair facing me.

I didn't feel I was being evaluated as much as I felt I was being enrolled.

"There will be others in the program with different addictions. Not all are alcoholics."

So I am alcoholic? Other than what I'd heard from Preacher Prince Harming, this was the beginning of my indoctrination to all things recovery. Including the diagnosis (alcoholic) and the disease (alcoholism).

Immediately I began reflecting.

I had heard the "name" alcoholic and used it when I was angry with my mother. But I associated it with her personality and the way she behaved when she got drunk, not based on how often she used alcohol or the volume she drank.

And I was so different than she was.

I didn't get angry and vicious when I drank. Well, not often, at least. Every now and again, I could be provoked by someone giving me a dirty look or calling me a name. If I was drunk I might find myself in a verbal conflict, but since I turned eighteen and could go to jail for it, I was less likely to get physical.

There was one Memorial Day with Sharina. We had been drinking all day at her house. We left the kids with the husbands for a beer run. Our beer runs typically turned into being out for the evening. First stop, the River Road House Tavern. We left after losing our asses in video poker. Next stop, Westwood a couple miles down the road. A gal said something snotty and rude and Sharina wouldn't side with me. We left. I wasn't able to let it go and my anger was redirected to my sister.

We didn't even make it to her place. She pulled over in the Fred Meyer parking lot just down the street from her house. I don't recall any punches thrown, but there was pulling, pushing and a lot of screaming. I took off into the bushes. Sharina went home. A concerned neighbor called the police. I was handcuffed and placed in the back of a police car where I continued to scream and act outraged.

Rex showed up with the boys in the car. I started to cry. I couldn't believe my babies were seeing me like this. The police released me to my husband and we went home. I was crying and remorseful. The next day was even worse. I hated putting all the pieces together in random order. Especially when I thought about Cody and Austin seeing me in the back of the police car handcuffed and acting belligerent.

Shame.

Every cell in my being was infected with shame.

But this was a rare and random act of violence. Sharina and I have been drinking buddies since our teens and I can count on one hand how many times we got in anything more than a verbal disagreement.

Not so with Prince Harming. He and I fought non-stop. Always. Though I was quick to retreat after that first beating, anger still raged inside me. I hated that I felt trapped and stuck with him.

But I wasn't an alcoholic, was I?

I didn't shift through so many emotions like Mom did. Not even with Prince Harming. I was either indifferent or angry. For me it was one or the other—no middle ground. There was no happy, silly, or even sad. I could sit in front of the television and drink eight to ten beers and not speak to a soul. I didn't have a need to talk to anyone or hash out any injustices. I just wanted numb.

And I never drank until I physically couldn't pick up another drink like she did. I didn't run away into the darkness and subject myself to rape and beatings. I did manage to find myself in a drunk tank. Oof. The horror. The embarrassment.

I went out to celebrate a co-workers birthday. We started at Tequila Willy's and a limo delivered us to two more bars. My next memory was being under the I-5 freeway overpass off SW Corbett Ave, near downtown Portland. I was yelling at some unseen instigators in the middle of the road. Covered with scratches up and down my legs from running through the ivy filled hillside at the freeway entrance a few blocks down. I was yelling at demons.

The cops showed up, handcuffed me and took me to the drunk tank. There I got to see myself in the faces of all the other drunkards. One gal's open sunburn wounds were covered in dirt. She held her arms and legs stiffly away from her body. Crying. Horrified, I began demanding for her to get help. They kept telling me if I would just calm down and be quiet I could go home. But I was outraged. Just call me Norma Rae of the drunk tank. Funny. Not funny?

Eventually I conceded to their recommendation to sit down and shut up and was released.

Of course, there is the matter of Prince Harming physically and mentally abusing me. I did make it my personal goal to get drunk enough not to care if he crawled on top of me. But I could have always had one more drink.

If I'd filled out that "Are you an alcoholic?" checklist, it would have looked like this.

How much do you drink? *A lot.*

Ever black out or lose time? *I have.*

Do you do things you normally wouldn't? *See Prince Harming.*

Yep, I've been alcoholic since I was 5 years old, hungover and playing with my Easy-Bake oven.

Maybe there is something to this alcoholism.

I agreed to start the program.

"Great!" Scott said as he reached out to shake my hand. Aside from the sense that he just closed a sale, I felt kind of hopeful. He handed me a couple pamphlets about alcoholism and recovery.

"I'll see you in class next week," he said as he checked his watch and escorted me through the door.

"Thank you, Scott." I tried expressing to him my appreciation by making eye contact, but he wasn't looking at me and seemed ready to move on, maybe to the next patient *(prospect)*?

When I saw Prince Harming, my hope and excitement ebbed just a little.

In the car, I was daydreaming about how life would be without alcohol. He was ready to go into his "let me tell you everything I know" role after I shared I had agreed to outpatient treatment. His voice was like the adults in the Peanuts cartoon: "wah-wah-wah."

Even my closest relationship, with Sharina, had always revolved around drinking. She was my drinking buddy. No one could drink with me like she could.

Wow! Just wow. What will that relationship be like? What will we do together? How will we relate? Talk? It's just weird to realize how much I had come to depend on alcohol as a buffer or connector.

Our work crews all drank and we provided the booze and the party space. Mike was one of our project leads and our drinking buddy. He was also my aunt's long-time boyfriend. This is the same couple that picked Prince Harming up and let him stay with them while I recovered from his beating. Our boozing it up served as a cushion and helped blur the lines for sloppy work and bad feelings, from both sides. My head reeled with all the possibilities and potential problems of living without alcohol.

Never fear, I could always be brought back into reality through the sermons of my personal preacher, Prince Harming. Ever the expert in all things recovery, "Believe Dat!"

I need a drink, I thought to myself as we merged on to I-205.

Funny. Not funny.

The night of the first class, I prepared just like I was going to a business meeting or dinner with friends. Hair done, full make up and dressed to impress. I walked in ready to make friends and do this! Whatever "this" was.

I was immediately aware of a more somber energy. Everybody had this kind of defeated mask on. Picture Eeyore from Winnie the Pooh, but a group of them. And here came Tigger, that's me, bouncing in with hope and optimism.

We went around the room and shared a little bit about ourselves. I followed the cadence of those who went before me and I blended into the group. "Hi. My name it Teresa, I'm alcoholic, I guess? I have been drinking a lot for a long time and I wanna stop."

Huh, I realized these people were desperately clinging to stay clean and sober. Their demeanor was intense, a little desperate, and their language definite.

Maybe I hadn't reached their point in recovery. It was probably that relapse thing that I had heard so much about. I was sure I would understand the longer I was in recovery.

Merging into group was pretty seamless. It wasn't a progressive process, where you start at class one and build on your lessons through twelve. So, you could integrate with the group at any point. Group members would start, quit or graduate every week. This design was brilliant because you didn't have to wait to get started. When you were ready, you could slide right in at any time.

There were two facilitators, Scott and Veronica. Compared to meek and mild Scott, Veronica was a peacock who drew the group's attention immediately. She would walk in the room straight and tall, she didn't give a lot of attention to her appearance. She had brown short hair with a natural wave, minimal makeup, an athletic build and a haughty manner.

She walked with a deliberate and no-nonsense stride. She didn't really look at anybody when she talked and her voice was very loud and clear, noticeably missing any empathy. She spoke with authority. Veronica talked at us more than engaging with us.

"How many times have you thought about drinking today? Two, maybe three times, maybe more? I don't have a magic word to remove your thoughts, so you need to pay attention in this class and hopefully hear something that can help you." Veronica instructed in a clear and measured tone. She walked around the group throwing disconnected glances like she was practicing for a speech in an empty room. There was no trace of emotion. Almost void of humanity.

Maybe she was just jaded working with people like us.

Scott went through the motions and followed Veronica's lead. He was just doing his job. That was fine with him. There did seem to be a bit more empathy from his side. I had noted to myself that if I needed someone to show me some understanding, I would definitely choose Scott.

Our group consisted of mostly alcoholics and a couple prescription addicts.

Harry shared about his love of getting drunk and how he would inevitably wake up into a relationship with a woman on any given bender. He was a hard worker and the drinking didn't keep him from being a good employee, but his personal life was a mess. His words.

Cathy was a very attractive mother and wife who

happened to live in my same small town of Silverton, OR. Cathy epitomized the "soccer mom."

"I stop at the liquor store and get a bottle of vodka at least once a day on my way home," she said. "Sometimes I don't even wait until I get home to open the bottle and start drinking. I have to hide it in different spots in the house. If my husband finds it, he'll dump it."

Her sparkling blue eyes were wide and looked desperate. She was speaking as if to get herself to listen. *If I don't quit drinking, my husband is going to leave me.*

Derek worked at the hospital and couldn't stop drinking. He was probably about 6' 4" and very attractive. If I passed him anywhere or met him outside of this room, I would have thought this guy had his shit together. He also used marijuana. His personal relationship was in jeopardy and he was on probation at work. He was very matter of fact. Concerted. Sharpened his pencils and sat in the front of the class to take copious notes, kind of guy.

Patty was addicted to "oxi-something or other". She was complaining, near crying: "It feels like my head is soft, like a sponge." Almost patting herself on the head, but careful not to make contact. "Like if you touch my head it's going to cave in. I feel like there are bugs crawling under my skin." Rocking back and forth, Patty was completely distracted. I had no idea how she was going to listen and take in anything they are trying teach us.

"Pay attention and hopefully you will hear something that can help you." Veronica's words from earlier flashed in my mind.

Wait, what was the "Oxi" med that was prescribed to me a few months ago for anxiety? Hmmm.

I felt so bad for all of them. I just wanted to take their pain away. I didn't feel desperate or helpless or out of control. I felt pretty solid about my decision to stop drinking.

But I knew and had been told time and again: relapse is part of recovery. I wait for the other shoe to drop.

We had different exercises to help us gain perspective and insight. Whatever that meant. The first was a lifeline to identify different painful events in our life. I drew a long horizontal line on the paper. To the left was when I was born and to the right was where I was then. I was supposed to indicate traumatic events and where they fell on my lifeline.

Wait, you want me to what? You want me to share with all of you, people I've just met, things that have cause me pain and trauma. For what, exactly?

I half-assed it at best. I haven't even spoken this kind of stuff to myself or my sister--no one. I wasn't going to open those memory files. Not there. Not then. I couldn't connect with my past. When I tried to call up what was available for access, the things I had remembered seemed irrelevant and quite frankly, embarrassing and shameful. Yep, those memories would stay right where they were.

But I was super interested in supporting the others. I appreciated their stories and their willingness to open their wounds. I was willing to observe and listen. The exchange of personal stories, the vulnerability we experienced and the common battle we were all fighting bonded us.

It was more of the same through the next several weeks. People came and went. But the core of the group remained intact, with the exception of Patty.

Patty didn't make it a month before she opted out of

treatment. She was suffering and there was little sympathy offered by Veronica and Scott. At least, not that I witnessed. I don't know that sympathy would have helped. I just felt her pain and thought she needed TLC instead of lifelines and journaling or drawing pictures of her feelings. It seemed she was not able to even concentrate enough for those thoughts to land. Let alone go digging for them.

One week we discussed getting support outside of the outpatient treatment program. Alcoholics Anonymous seemed to be the "go-to." It seemed all the group members had been to an AA meeting. Veronica was quick to share her dislike of AA. "I won't elaborate now, but if you make it through your twelve weeks, I'll tell you my story."

What a bitch. Like she's dangling a carrot or something.

I had no knowledge of AA, with the exception of the one meeting we attended so Prince Harming could get a slip signed for his parole officer. We didn't stay for the entire meeting. Then he started signing them himself. That was my one and only AA experience.

Harry was a die-hard member. He talked about his

preference for closed AA meetings—only alcoholics allowed. He liked when it was mostly the old-timers and couldn't stand the newbies: "They always think they know everything" Harry was an older guy. Likable. Super nice. Short, black groomed hair. Darker somewhat weathered skin, maybe Spanish or Native American descent. He looked tired, didn't smile much at first and his hands shook. But when he did smile he was very handsome. Instant facelift.

Harry gave me an amethyst necklace. "It's a belief among my people that the amethyst will keep you from getting drunk." The stone was a natural cut, not polished or shaped, strung on a simple leather choker.

How sweet and interesting that he's giving this to me. But if you believe in this, why don't you keep it for yourself? Why hasn't it worked for you?

I graciously accepted his gift and didn't share with him my questioning thoughts.

One night when Prince Harming came to pick me up he let my little Shih Tzu, Daisy, out of the Blazer. The whole group was downstairs smoking and Derek teased, "It figures you'd have a dog like that."

They all laughed and gestured in agreement. Daisy was all dressed up in bows and looking her best. Kind of like how I showed up at the first class. Well, all the classes. It was cute. I felt a little loved being teased by my brothers and sisters.

When I got in the car, Prince Harming was cold and demanding: "Did any of those guys hit on you? Which one is Harry?"

He had not been a fan of the gift. Boy, he knew how to fuck up a good moment.

"Of course, none of them are interested in me for anything other than our group," I snapped. I was so offended because I saw the pain in these men. I never even considered they would be thinking anything else besides "I hope this works this time."

Maybe I was naïve.

"Which one is the guy who gave you the necklace?" Prince Harming barks, trying to catch me in a lie.

"I told you, Harry. He isn't here."

"What's that guy's deal?" He nodded in the direction of Derek.

"What do you mean--He's in treatment!"

Prince Harming was with me night and day. Day after day. The only time we were apart was when he dropped me off two minutes before treatment and was there waiting when I walk out. I wouldn't be surprised if he came walking into the conference room to be introduced as the new kid in class. Not because he wanted to be a better and healthier human being, but because he wanted to be part of something he was not the center of. Because he needed to know what was going on with me 24-7.

Many of the group members had to do urine tests for work or another agency. Or like Cathy, they were trying to save their marriage. I was the only one there purely because of my desire to stop drinking. I wasn't sent by anyone or given an ultimatum.

And I quickly learned from them that, since it was my first try, my odds for staying sober were very, very slim.

"Recovery is a lifelong process and you can pretty much count on relapse. It's likely that you'll have to practice for a while before getting sober," Scott proclaimed with an air of boredom.

CHAPTER SEVEN

Alcoholics Anonymous

"Habit is habit, and not to be flung out of the window by any man, but coaxed down-stairs one step at a time."

— Mark Twain

I was coming up on sixty days completely abstinent from all alcohol. This was a big deal. With the exception of my two pregnancies, Cody in 1985 and Austin in 1989-90, I had never gone longer than a few days without a drink. The really bizarre thing was that it had been relatively easy.

I had opted not to see my sister during this time. Her husband and Prince Harming were friends and got along well, but I just couldn't see us doing anything other than drinking together. We had partied every weekend for the last couple years up until two months prior. Our kids had even come to expect and then missed these little gatherings.

Life had been pretty boring, but sober. Prince Harming suggested we go to an AA meeting that weekend. Okay, it was kind of out of the blue, but I figured what the hell? I was game. He told me there was a Saturday morning meeting just a few blocks down the street. I found it interesting that he had done his homework. Oh, well, I agreed to go.

It was a beautiful Saturday morning and I was up early. I was not terribly excited to go to an AA meeting. The one and only meeting I had attended didn't seem all that interesting and I felt out of place.

It was in a back room at a big pink church in Oregon City, with standing room only. I remembered them making space up front for us because we were new. *How did they know we were new?* It was really awkward because we were just there to get Prince Harming's slip signed and weren't going to stay. But not wanting to disrupt the meeting any more than we had, we accepted the seats they offered. We cut out before the meeting was over.

Perhaps I'd feel different now that I had been diagnosed as alcoholic by the outpatient treatment program.

"What do you wear to an AA meeting?" I asked Prince Harming. Not wanting to feel out of place any more than I already assumed I would. Veronica's judgment about AA popped in my head. He explained they are all different and suggested a nice pair of pants and heels.

Why didn't I pay better attention to what women were wearing at the meeting we went to a few months back? What kind of people were going to be there? I imagined a room full of Harry's—shaky-handed older men who don't smile. Sneering and hating the newbies.

Mental note: Remember Harry said he hated the newbies because they thought they knew too much…don't know too much!

I dressed business casual with full makeup and hair, and walked to the front door of "my" first AA meeting. We had to walk through the restaurant to get to the banquet room where the meeting was held. Nice! Nothing like walking through a full restaurant with a scarlet A on your forehead.

Tables lined the room with seating facing the middle so everybody was visible to each other. There was no hiding there. The waitress came around to take orders and I passed, thank you. I didn't know if I belonged there.

But Prince Harming seemed to be in his element and chatted it up with everybody. I overheard him talking about this was his first meeting in his hometown.

Your hometown? We just moved here seven months ago. Why are you acting like you've been going to meetings?

I continued to observe the room. There was a lot of loud chatter amongst a few older guys that looked real tired, and a handful or so around our age, mid-

30s. A crossed from us was this handsome older, 50s or 60s, couple who seemed almost regal. They were sitting straight and tall and perused the room as if to identify anyone who may be there to sully the kingdom. A younger man, late 20s or early 30s, sat between them like he was lost or their little boy. He had brown ringlets of hair and his shoulders slumped as he looked down at his hands. I wondered if he was twiddling his thumbs?

The whole scene seemed odd. Almost surreal. I felt like I had been dropped in a bad movie about alcoholism.

 (scene) Cue the music. Farrah Fawcett is made ugly and she enters the room. She's here trying to get sober to save her family. (end scene)

This happens every week? I wondered if all these people came week after week after week? Ate the same breakfast, watched the newbies come in and tell the old-timers how it's done, like Harry so hated. I wondered if I was the only newbie, since this was Prince Harming's first meeting in his hometown.

They opened the meeting with reading the twelve steps followed by the twelve traditions. They then asked if anyone had a birthday and Prince Harming said he had sixty days. I was shocked.

First, *what was a birthday*? Second, never once in the 59 days since I had drank had he copped to having any issues with alcohol.

He went on to introduce himself: "Hello, my name is Prince Harming, and I'm an alcoholic." They handed him a plastic coin that said "one month" and "To thine own self be true."

Ummm, check please. I about fell out of my seat.

He told the room that I had a birthday too, but I said my birthday is not until tomorrow and declined the chip.

They asked if I'd like to share and following the format I said:

"Hello, my name is Teresa and I'm an alcoholic."

Wow. I'm an alcoholic.

After that admission cleared my throat, I went on to say something like:

"This is the first time I've been sober and I'm prepared to draw my sword and slay the dragon if needed to stay sober, I am resolved. Thanks."

There were a couple nods, but most eyes averted and looked for anyone else who wanted to share.

I couldn't believe I didn't get a standing ovation for my declaration. I thought it was a pretty wicked analogy. Oh well, not my people. I was certain of my sobriety and no one could tell me different.

The man from the regal pair, Dan, shared about how the younger man sitting between them, Rich, was back again. "He's been struggling, but at least he's back. I'm glad he's here." I liked this. They really cared about this guy. That was cool.

I heard a lot of sadness and there were a few laughs. The breakfast looked good. I may come back. I thought, maybe. It wasn't so bad, Veronica. It was funny that I thought of her. It wasn't horrible. I was kind of excited to see the outpatient group and share my experience.

In preparing to close the meeting we all held hands and recited the serenity prayer, which sounded pretty good. Something along the lines of "Give me serenity and help to accept things that can't be changed and help us to be brave and wise to change what needs to be changed"

And then they chanted: "Keep coming back--It works if you work it."

Okay, back to, cue-the-music, bad-movie moment.

According to my newly (almost) sixty-days sober alcoholic boyfriend, "The chant means, if you work the program, do everything as instructed, it will work to keep YOU sober." He directed it right at me.

Keep me sober? What about YOUR sobriety? I thought.

"Well, I'm already sober," I said.

"What if you drink?"

"What do you mean, what if I drink? Why would I drink?" I was getting irritated as we moved through the thick of people trying to get out of the restaurant.

"Nobody just *gets* sober. You have to have a program."

"You mean I have to go to AA to stay sober?" What an insolent suggestion.

In truth, I felt very comfortable the way I was living

sober. I was choosing my battles because I just didn't care about fighting with him. I felt more of ME in these last couple of months than I had in years. Why mess with what had been working?

"I'll think about it," I said.

"I'll be right back." He walked over to Dan.

"What's with the card? Is it his business card?" I asked as he returned. I was concerned with what he might be stirring up.

"No, actually, it's really smart." He handed it to me. "It has his name and number to make it easier than trying to find paper and pen."

"Hmmm…makes sense." I shrugged my shoulders and walk to the car door.

Prince Harming was saying his goodbyes and acted like he was one of the gang. *Whatever.*

We ran a couple errands and went home. I had been trying to be more active by taking walks and getting on my treadmill. It was so nice out, warm and sunny, we took the dogs to the high school field and walked the track a few times.

"Why don't we have your sister and Ken over tonight?"

"Absolutely not. I don't feel comfortable with them coming over yet. They are too connected to the old partying ways. What would we do?"

He said nothing.

"I'm going to lay down. Come on, girls." I called to the dogs and lay across the bed. Thankful he decided to stay up.

I woke late in the afternoon. Prince Harming peeked his head in the bedroom talking sickly sweet, "Wake up, sleepy eyes. It's time to get up."

"What's up?" My defense was activated and I waited.

"Sharina and Kenny are on their way."

What the fuck?

"I told you I didn't want them over. Why would you do that?"

He ignored me. Almost singing as he went down the stairs. "They'll be here any minute."

And it was on. I felt like a ticking time bomb. Tick,

tick, tick, tick, tick.

What were we going to do sober? How do we act? I'm just getting to know me sober. And you, Prince Harming, are getting more despicable with every passing day. My mind was spinning.

Do I leave? Do I stay? I loved my sister. The boys were excited to see their cousins and have everybody over. They missed our parties.

They pulled up and I gripped myself internally. *Here we go.* I wasn't sure what to expect. I put on my best smile and tried with all my might to act normal. *What's normal?* I wondered. Because normal was new to me, I probably looked anything but. Typically, we would have barbequed and karaoked with beer flowing. I had no interest in karaoke. I didn't want to sing and I didn't want to hear them sing. I wondered if Prince Harming was still sober? Or was he planning on drinking with them? Was that the plan for them to drink and I would just be sober?

It was awkward. So awkward. I felt like everybody was watching and waiting for me to decide how to act or what to do. Prince Harming decided we should all go bowling. It was a nice intervention to shift the focus and energy off of me. The problem with bowling is it was one of our old drinking past times.

At the bowling alley, I still felt like everybody was waiting for me to make a move. Like they were waiting for me to get the party started. I was so distracted with the intense pressure of "what's she going to do," I wasn't even present in the moment of sobriety I did have while bowling. I wasn't talking and I couldn't relax. I was avoiding eye contact, because I was afraid I would lash out. "What the fuck do you want from me? If you want me to drink, just say so!"

About an hour into our game I decided screw it, and went up and ordered a beer. They followed suit. I was pissed. I didn't want to drink. I felt like I was carrying this weight and had to drink so they could drink and we could all act "normal." I didn't feel normal with the first or the second beer. The third went down easier, but it still didn't feel right.

We walked home and the sky was beautiful and clear. Stars filled the dark blue canvas. The kids were laughing and talking running ahead. I was still kind of on edge, but tried to engage in small talk. *Who was I? What did this mean?* I was trying desperately to shut down the shame and disappointment that had moved in to my mind. My sister was quiet and clearly uncomfortable. I wondered if she was disappointed in me?

As we approached the house, Sharina said, "We're just going to head home."

"Okay." Home? What an interesting thought. *I wished I could go home.*

Prince Harming was his normal loud and obnoxious self. "I'll call you tomorrow, man. See ya!" he yelled as he ran in to grab the keys for the van. He made a beer run and brought back a six-pack. I might have drunk one beer, maybe two, but no more than that. I left beer in the refrigerator. That hadn't happened in over two years. I went to bed.

When I woke up on Sunday, March 3rd, what would have been my sixty days sober, I realized that, according to the world of recovery and my very own in-house guru, my number of sober days had just been reset.

I was a fucking loser. I failed. I failed and I hadn't even wanted to drink. I hated myself. I hated that I succumbed to the pressure. If I drank when I didn't even want to what did that mean about my ability to live sober? To have any control over my life?

What I couldn't see then was the manipulation. I grabbed a notebook and scribbled the following letter.

March 3, 2003

I'm just gonna start writing and whatever I'm feeling or thinking will be here. I don't know where to go from here. I feel lost, sad, weak, hopeless, helpless, mad, dumb, stupid, and the list goes on. I didn't want to get out of bed today. Because I knew when I did I would have to face what I did. I would like to say that I regret it…it's hard to use regret when you purposely, willfully made a conscious decision to move backwards. To take my progress, my could-be victory and trash it. For what!!! a sour stomach, a pounding headache, a feeling of deep despair in my soul. I am purposely not using your name as I hate it, you with every fiber of my being. I learned to love me again in the last few months and I was at peace with myself and my choices in life. I can't imagine what I see in you? You are revolting! I accepted you last night with distaste but I knew after an hour or so I would loosen up and I did. However, I felt inadequate this time. I wasn't completely accepting of you and what you brought out in me this time. I know how you got to me. I know that you are very resourceful in your seduction. Well know this!! You mother fucker! You are going to have to come to terms with the fact that I am aware of your deceptions, I do loathe you, I am willing to go toe to toe with you and I am getting stronger! I will train and I WILL DEFEAT YOU! You won this battle, but you won't win the WAR!

Teresa L. Martin

3/3/03

I knew I consciously wrote the letter to alcohol, but I couldn't help think I was writing to the devil in my bed.

I was pretty much inconsolable. I didn't know how much it was about the alcohol and how much it was about him.

He called Dan and told him the news that he just relapsed.

Poor baby. You just became an alcoholic yesterday.

That gained him an invitation to the Sunday night

meeting just outside of town. I was such a wreck, I agreed to go with him. He was right. They were all right. I HAD to relapse. I wondered how many times I would have to do this before I would ever get to be sober?

The weather was as gloomy as my mood. Yesterday had been so sunny, bright and beautiful. You could feel spring in the air. Tonight the clouds sat low and heavy with rain. Just like my soul.

We pulled up to a small white church. Several people huddled under an awning to smoke, others were entering the front doors, and one or two people touched nearly everyone that walked past them with either a hug or a handshake. I was numb. I had no other option. This was my last hope.

I got out of the Blazer and walked toward the doors. I ducked around another person so I didn't get hugged. If someone would have hugged me right then I would have shattered.

I walked in the doors, found a seat in the back and started to cry. I cried damn near through the entire meeting, which was over an hour long.

What the fuck am I going to do? Am I really that

broken that I can't stay sober? I can't believe this. I am so confused.

I knew that sobriety was my only chance at living. I simply couldn't go on living life the way I had the last few years. My life sucked. I had to quit drinking.

The meeting was pretty much the same as the one the morning before.

So much changed within forty-eight hours. Bea, Dan's regal wife, came over to me and said, "It's okay if you want to call me and talk."

She was lovely, sweet and I believed she wanted to help. Her confidence and assuredness was attractive.

Her frosted highlights complemented her greying long loose braided hair that fell over her shoulder. She had tanned skin and a straight white smile. She wore thick black rimmed glasses, but that didn't take away from her beauty. She was dressed casual with cropped jeans, and a white t-shirt type top with a boat neckline. She wore simple jewelry, a dainty necklace and earrings. Her clothes were pressed, which gave the casual attire a more polished look. She moved with an air of comfort in her own skin and seemed to know everybody.

I wanted what she had.

On our way home I was quiet and Prince Harming started non-stop talking about what he thought of the meeting.

"Bea seems real nice. It's a good meeting. I think we should make this our home meeting. It's going to be okay, babe. Don't worry about it, everybody relapses. It's part of the road to recovery. I like Dan. I'm going to ask him to be my sponsor. I think you should ask Bea to be your sponsor. It's all going to work out."

I was in a daze and couldn't believe the turn of events. *Who the fuck was I?*

What was a home group? Sponsor? What the hell was that? I blinked into his endless prattle, but didn't say a word.

I was quiet, stuck in my head. Shell-shocked by the last two days. Everything I felt so sure about, poof, just like that, gone. I was swimming in a sea of disbelief and worry.

What now?

CHAPTER EIGHT

GOD

One day at a time

When I opened my eyes, the sun was back. The big, full windows in our second floor master bedroom flooded the room with light.

What's that? A little bit of hope? Thank goodness.

I jumped out of bed and headed downstairs to start the coffee. I went to my coat and pulled out the piece of paper with Bea's name and number. I carried it around with me as if willing it to inspire me to call. It worked. I grabbed the phone and snuck off to a quiet corner.

Where was he anyway? It occurred to me I hadn't seen Prince Harming yet that morning. And just like that I didn't care.

"Hello," I said when she answered the phone. "We met last night. I'm the woman that was sitting in the back, you came over and…" She chuckled and said, "Yes, I know who this is."

I let out an exhale of relief. The awkward beginning was out of the way.

I explained I didn't know anything about AA and I wasn't sure what a sponsor was or did, but Prince Harming suggested I gave her a call. I didn't know what else to do, so there I was.

"Do you want to stop drinking? "

I answered with an emphatic yes.

She suggested I get a Big Book and start reading. She explained there were twelve steps and an action to be taken with each step. I started freaking out, asking "What if I can't do this?"

"Just take it one day at a time," she said. Okay. Deal.

Prince Harming came back with donuts and Starbucks. He mouthed, "Is that Bea on the phone?" and I nodded. He seemed pleased. Call me an asshole, but something about pleasing him displeased me. He sat down the coffee next to me, kissed me on the head and stepped outside on the deck with his phone. I knew he was calling Dan. I was a bit annoyed he was calling right after I called Bea, but whatever. I fell back into my indifferent mode instead of questioning him.

I couldn't help but feel set up.

When he came in a few minutes later he was wearing a huge grin and damn near skipping. He seemed almost proud of himself.

What was this all about?

I found a daily meeting held at a church up the road and we checked it out. We, yes we! Me and my shadow walked through the halls to a small conference room where there were just two others. Max, an average looking man. Father of two and worked to put food on the table, said he had two years sober. After experiencing a near meltdown losing 59 days sober, I couldn't imagine what having two years would be like. He stopped me: "Take it one day at a time." Funny, that's what Bea said. When the other gal started sharing I was surprised to find she was there for overeating. She said she needed a meeting. I had no idea there was an Overeaters Anonymous and would have never guessed someone would come to an AA meeting with a food habit? It seemed so trivial to me back then.

It had come time for me to go back to my weekly class with outpatient treatment. I felt like I was cheating on them.

But this was about getting outside support. Maybe Veronica's opinion mattered to me more than I thought it did?

That night, as we were driving back from a worksite, I mentioned, "I need to get ready for class tonight."

Prince Harming seemed surprised that I was going back to class. He whipped out the book of AA meetings. "I thought we'd go to a new meeting tonight," he said. "Look, this is the one Dan and Bea go to. It's a few towns away. Come on, let's do this together."

"I'm not comfortable just bailing out like this. Like I'm hiding. I need to at least call."

"Call them now." He handed me the cell phone.

I grabbed the phone and dialed. Great, Veronica picks up.

"Hi, it's Teresa."

"Yah, what do you need?"

"I had a few beers last weekend and went to an AA meeting the next day."

Silence.

"I found a sponsor and have been talking with her. She has 15 years sober."

"Okay?"

"Well, I'm just going to work a program through AA. I'm going to miss everybody…"

"Alright, I'll let Scott know you won't be back." She sounded annoyed. But she always sounded annoyed.

"Goodbye." I said. A little annoyed and a little sad. Not about Veronica, but the group.

Click. This was the end of my outpatient treatment.

I talked regularly with Bea and was working my Twelve Steps of Alcoholics Anonymous.

I admitted I was powerless over alcohol. Being a woman who sought control by being tough and taking the position of I don't give a shit, this was not comfortable, but I wanted change more than I wanted to fight the system. Fine. I'm powerless.

I came to believe a higher power could restore my sanity. Not that I ever had any sanity to restore. Just trying to survive my life had made me pretty insane.

The third step required me to turn my life over to a God of my understanding. OK, now this was getting interesting. I had abandoned God at summer camp many years ago. Ummm, the God I understood probably wasn't too happy with me, and he was angry and vengeful. But I wasn't going to argue. I wanted to keep it moving.

With no passion in my heart I spoke the words. "I turn my life over to the God of my understanding."

I went to a meeting every day. Sometimes twice. There's a suggestion to go to ninety meetings in ninety days. I went to well over one hundred.

Nothing was taking my sobriety away this time.

NOTHING.

I received my thirty-day chip. It was kind of silly, but kind of cool too. Since I'd never gotten a lot of positive feedback, I wasn't comfortable with acknowledgement of my work or efforts. I mean I had some pretty rock-star work references that gave me glowing reviews, but nothing publicly. If someone would start to praise me, I would push it away and minimize it or tell a joke. Receiving just wasn't in my comfort zone.

I was like an attention- and love-starved toddler. I

wanted nothing more than to please Bea. She was amazing and I still wanted what she had. I wanted that peace. I wanted that full life. I wanted to be comfortable in my own skin. I wanted happily ever after.

Tuesday night was an all-women's group that I adored. Wonder why? You guessed it. I was all by myself with my newest and closest friends. No Prince Harming to check what I was saying or doing.

The Sunday night meeting was a regular meeting for us. But I never officially declared a home meeting. I had different attachments to the weekday noon meeting and the Sunday night meeting. Max had to go back to work and I stepped up to be at the weekday noon meeting every day. The Sunday meeting was where most of my "friends" attended. I did service work and was on the call list. I was committed to attending both meetings. Nobody ever pressed the issue. So, I remained homeless.

One Sunday, a guy walked in and sat in front of us. He was clearly upset. He had gone out drinking again. I recognized him as the one who sat between Dan and Bea at that first breakfast meeting a month or so ago. Poor bastard. He was so down.

Next thing I knew, Prince Harming was pulling out a business card. On it, I could see the name, Prince Harming Martin.

O M G. He had used my last name when first meeting customers so they didn't get confused, but this, lying to people in AA, was...I don't know what it was. He was lying. It wasn't the truth. Why did he have a business card? What's the point of the full name? When I was drinking I was too tired to push back on his lies and conman ways. But a large part of the AA program was about being rigorously honest. Not to mention he was only five or six weeks sober. What was he going to offer this guy? He had always been capable of just about anything. But, what was his angle now?

We continued to go through the motions. I soon realized that AA was just a ploy to keep me away from the situation that he had limited access to, outpatient treatment. Whereas he could attend every AA meeting with me and know what was going on at all times. He thought he could shape and mold me through his extensive knowledge of the program.

What he didn't factor was the influence and friendship of my sponsor. And that sobriety meant more than not drinking. I was waking up.

She never advised me about my relationship, but watching how she handled herself was an influence. She was a take-no-shit kind of woman—in a more powerful way than I had been. She had a good and loving relationship with her husband, Dan. They seemed fair and concerned with each other's happiness. I became much calmer at home and conversations with Prince Harming were more peaceful.

Until I brought up his lies.

About six weeks into my AA program, as the owner of our construction company, I received a notice to garner Prince Harming's wages. Wait for it: another child. The child was about to turn eighteen, but he owed in arrears and until said minor did turn eighteen he needed to pay. Under the influence of my sweet, calm sponsor I didn't lose my cool. But I didn't really know what to do either.

He seemed to be getting more agitated the longer we were sober. Instead of intimidating or out-yelling me, he would clinch his teeth, slam his phone down, and storm off. His fuse was shorter. Or maybe it was me.

I wasn't accepting his bullshit and didn't just shut down and allow his lies to fill the room. I figured he just wasn't working his program. None of my business. I wasn't about to "take his inventory"—telling him how he should work his program. As they say not to do. It was my permission not to care.

After all those high-earning years, our business was hurting. We hadn't received many work orders from the banks or been paid on invoices from our biggest client in almost two months. Something was happening. Maybe this was contributing to Prince Harming's restlessness.

And then we received news by letter—our biggest client was filing bankruptcy. We had over eighty thousand dollars out in invoicing to them. Which meant we had tens of thousands owed to vendors and workers. Not to mention our own personal bills. We were not good business people. We had no accounting practice in place and had yet to file taxes for 2001 or 2002.

I say we, but the fact was, it was just me. It was all in my name. I had 100% liability to repay debts and responsibility to take care of employees. Even with the proverbial noose around my neck, I wasn't going to drink.

Without the beer to numb me, I could feel a mighty storm brewing.

For my fourth step, I had to take a fearless moral inventory of myself. Bea told me to write it out in my own time. I grabbed an old pad and scribbled down some experiences that I had hated. Like being touched and fondled my entire childhood. I wrote about things that made me feel less than. Dirty. Damaged. I held the pen tightly and my writing was crude. Not recognizable. When I completed it we arranged for her to pick me up and she took me to her home where we could have complete privacy.

She went through the first three steps with me. We got on our knees and together prayed to turn my life over to God. It was nice and it made me feel closer to Bea, but not to God.

And then we got to the fourth step. Now, this is supposedly a pretty rough one. I don't know if it was because I was so ready to move forward or if I just wasn't spiritually or mentally able to go deep enough, but doing it didn't bother me so much.

I was ready to let go of some pretty awful secrets that

I thought might be the key to setting me free. I cried and hugged her. She was the first person I shared these awful events with. I didn't feel judged. I felt she listened with a sympathetic heart.

And in reflecting on what I shared with her, I believe I got the entire step wrong. I didn't take a fearless and moral inventory of myself. I simply shared some pretty shitty things that happened to me as a little girl and growing up.

Perhaps I missed an opportunity? But she didn't say anything, so maybe it was open for interpretation.

On the way home Bea had asked if I smoked and I said no. She asked if I was dieting and I said no. I went on, "I'm giving sobriety all of me."

She was super pleased to hear that. She said that many times when she brings on a new sponsee they want to change everything right now. Although I knew I wanted my body back, it wasn't even on my radar at this point. I wanted my life back. She had checked in about my relationship and I told her I didn't know about it. Again, I didn't care. I didn't care about him or us. My priority was to get me back.

When I got home Prince Harming came creeping

around the corner. He asked how it went. I told him it was good. I felt really good. As I was looking for a coffee can or anything I could burn my fourth step in, he started telling me what was going to happen next.

"You're going to need to take an inventory of all your character flaws and defects."

"Well, I want to talk about YOUR character defects. Specifically, the lying. If you ever want to have peace you're going to have to come clean about everything…"

I didn't know if there was anything left, but the lies hadn't stopped. I couldn't even remember how many kids we were at now—eight maybe nine? I should have received the Nobel Peace Prize just for getting this guy neutered.

He was angry that his bullying ways weren't working anymore. I would simply disengage when he started in on me. To add to that, I had a local community that he wasn't able to woo with his charms. I don't think it was that they didn't like him; he just wasn't able to "bullshit" them the way he was accustomed to doing.

He took off that night and I went to bed not caring where he went or if he was coming back. The next morning, he came upstairs with coffee. He was pleasant, but still gave me a creep factor.

Then he began to berate me, "You're out of line for telling me how to work my program! Who do you think you are? What are you some kind of expert now?" He was yelling at me like he couldn't believe I wasn't yielding. His desperation was growing.

My heart tightened. This man is unstable. Even though I felt he was completely losing his mind I stood by my statement and kept saying, "You will never have peace until you come clean one hundred percent."

He was livid.

There was a look in his eyes I hadn't seen before. Not even the night he pummeled my face with his fists. I had felt somewhat safe since I had been sober. Instead of engaging his lies and rants I would state my position and let it lie. I had no interest in arguing. I think this unnerved him. But now. Now, I was pushing back forcefully and not letting up. I held my position. He seemed desperate and that did scare me.

I sat down my coffee and grabbed my clothes as I

walked across the room. I dressed on my way downstairs and through the house to get in my Blazer. I drove to my mom's house. She called my sister.

I was hysterical.

"I can't keep pretending everything is okay. I can't. I hate him and I'm never going to be free of him. He's never going to go away," I sobbed.

I said right then that I was going to either die by his hand or he was going to have to find someone else to hook on to. One of these two options would be my only escape from this man. I knew it to my soul I wasn't ever going to be free. I couldn't wish this man on anybody else. I felt doomed. As much as my mom and sister wanted to console me—they knew there was little they could say or do. They cried with me and assured me they were there if I needed anything...

On my way home I cried and cried. Even though I went through the motions of the whole God thing, steps one through three, I felt no spiritual connection and had no belief that He would listen to me.

But I was done. I didn't know what that meant

exactly, I just knew I was.

As I drove along Highway 99 I started ripping off my expensive acrylic nails. Each one left my nail bed stripped and incredibly sensitive to touch. Painful. Spitting out chips of nail, I called my hairdresser and told her I wouldn't be coming for my regular appointments any longer and to cancel whatever was on the books. I was gasping between sobs.

I didn't know what I was doing, I was just making change. It's all I felt I could do. These things just didn't matter any longer.

I pulled up to the house. It seemed quiet. All the vehicles were accounted for. I walked in. No television on.

"Hello?!" I yelled. I walked through the bottom floor. You would think I would be afraid, but I wasn't.

When I got upstairs, I dropped to my knees.

For the first time in my life I felt completely raw and naked. My soul was exposed. I splayed my arms, threw my head back and I prayed to God like I had never prayed. I opened my heart and I pleaded, "Please God forgive me. I need you. Please restore to me my peace. Help me. Please." I held there for several moments...surrendering.

I raised my head and through tears and wails, I noticed a few of the travel bags were out on the bed. I turned around and saw hangers on the floor. I wiped my face with my hands and I grabbed my cell phone.

What? Where is he? My mind raced. I ran to the closet. Sure enough clothes were gone. No way!

I called Prince Harming, my whole being shaking. But with a cool and measured voice, I asked, "Where are you?

"I'm at the airport. I'm going to my mom's for a few days," he said.

FREEDOM.

"Oh no, you're not coming back. You are not coming back! I am changing every lock in the house, and if you dare, I will have you arrested!"

I hung up and called my uncle and asked him to come over as soon as possible to change the locks on all the doors. I was stunned. Shocked. *Could this be true?* I could have never in a million years dreamed...I would have never dared to even wish...

for him to be removed that instantly from my life.

I waited for the other shoe to drop. I waited for him to show up and demand to be let in. Maybe he would break down the door and beat me to death this time.

But he didn't.

The one thing I had going for me was he knew sober me didn't use a lot of words and didn't make empty promises. I didn't engage. I engaged this time!

Now when I think of this day, I picture God picking him up by the scruff of his neck and removing him from my life. I wish I could say that was the end of it and I lived happily ever after.

Unfortunately, there was still a large system coming through.

Batten down the hatches.

PART THREE

PINK CLOUDS

The storm broke.

The fog cleared.

With a little love from the sun,

the clouds blushed shades of pink.

CHAPTER NINE

Reckoning

Life isn't about waiting for the storm to pass. It's about learning to dance in the rain.

April 26. I've been sober about six weeks.

"What do you mean I have no money in the account? I'm overdrawn?"

Brett's jaw was rigid, not budging, but his eyes were soft. "Looks like a check was written against the account that probably caused the overdrafts. It was made out to Prince Harming Martin," the bank manager said.

That son of a bitch.

I told Brett I had never written a check to my ex and if it's signed, he forged the signature.

"Please come into my office," Brett said as he gestured for me to follow him. Tears were brimming, but I refused to cry over this monster any longer.

I followed him to his office and we sat down. "You can go after Mr. Martin," Brett started.

I cut him off. "His name is not Mr. Martin. It's Mr. Harming," I said through gritted teeth. "And didn't you ask for identification?" "Ms. Martin, he's been in and out of here with and without you over the last six months. We have rarely asked either of you for your identification. We strive to develop strong relationships with our customers. We felt we were conducting business as usual with your account." He went on, "Your only recourse is to call the police and file a report. In the end, you'll need to sue Mr. Harming for the funds."

My response:

A. That doesn't help me now. I'm broke.

B. I'm done with this bastard!

My face was hot and I wanted to scream. I could feel my breath ragged and short. My body was shaking and I had visions of Prince Harming being executed in my head. Oh, the anger seethed in me.

This despicable human being. How could I have been so foolish? I knew. I knew all along he was a conman, a liar and a thief. Did I really think I was anything more than a target? Of course he would empty the bank account...

What do I do now?

I need a meeting, I thought, on purpose. What I was really thinking was I need to numb out. But I opted not to do either.

I chose retaliation.

Prince Harming still had the company cell phone, but I didn't bother calling him about the money. For what? So he could lie and tell me the check's in the mail? Or that he'd pay me back? He's sorry? He was a bottomless pit of deceit.

I did want to hurt him any way I could, so I cut his phone service off.

The next call came from his mom's number in California. He was pissed alright.

"Who the fuck do you think you are?" he screamed at me.

I just listened as he bellowed obscenities. Too bad. I had other things to focus on and I needed to get the rage out of my system. I knew cutting the phone off would poke the beast. It felt good. I took a little bit of my power back in that one small step.

Of course, being terrified of the desperate sociopath's ability to cover distance by air or road, I did want to maintain some communication with him. Just so I knew where he was. I wasn't foolish enough to believe that I was safe yet.

A couple of checks from outstanding invoices were scheduled to come in anytime and I prayed he wouldn't figure out a way to re-route them to where he was. Thankfully he didn't and I managed to stay afloat for a week or two.

But I knew I was right in the middle of a huge financial storm and I had no idea how I was going to survive it.

Prince Harming was the skill and resource for directing others to do the construction work properly. Without him and our primary account, there was no construction company.

As a licensed contractor I could still do clean outs, which involved removing all the former tenant's property—garbage, furniture, pet and human waste. Your average everyday dream job. I also still had my dealer's license; I could sell used manufactured homes. But there wasn't much of a buyers' market because the massive numbers of homes being repossessed meant you couldn't get financed for them. Unless you had a cash buyer, you were out of luck.

In mid-May I got a call from Don at Mutual Bank. He

asked for Prince Harming and I told him he was no longer with the company. He said he had a new repo that needed to be cleaned out and cleaned up. I took the details and surveyed the job to give an appropriate estimate. Just as I always did. A lot of these homes needed a large U-Haul to dispose of destroyed appliances and furniture, mountains of garbage, bad carpeting, and more. There were times I had to clean out shower stalls used for cat boxes, and pick up human feces left throughout the house.

I'd seen better and I'd seen worse than this one. I sent him a formal bid and took a deep breath. I waited. I wanted nothing more than to walk away from all things connected to Prince Harming. There was a part of me that knew as long as I was still involved with this work, his ghost would always be there tormenting me with the threat he might return. This industry is what he knew.

But this was a simple way to generate some income, right?

I was torn because while I hated this work and this business, it was all I knew at the time. And I could bid and clean in my sleep.

It took about a week to hear I got the job. I talked with Bea about the new opportunity and was a little surprised when she said she'd like to make some "play" money for herself. Play money was just for Bea. She could spend it any way she liked and didn't have to add it to the house account. And it helped that she would wait until I was paid to be paid.

We got to the house and it was evident the past tenants were not happy about leaving. Garbage and rotten food filled one of the bathtubs. Dried raw egg was everywhere. I can still smell the stench of rotten egg and milk. I was grateful for having a job and got to work. I needed some muscle to help me load and dump some larger items, so I asked a few people at my noon meeting who I knew were between jobs. They were glad to lend a hand.

It had been a long time since I had a sense of community. I felt blessed. Such support and healthy friendships had been absent for nearly a decade— since just before I got involved with Tory, my old married boss.

I took digital photos to show the work order was complete and sent them over with an invoice. I prayed it all would go smoothly and I'd get paid sooner than later. The money wasn't great, but it would help.

Weeks went by without hearing from Don with new job prospects.

Creditors called every day. Many were vendors we got materials from for the rehab work. Some were employees who needed their final pay and others who needed more work. Some were customers that Prince Harming had taken private contracts for work. And one was calling about a van we had sold and they were waiting for the title because the loan had not been paid to clear it. Most of them were people I had never talked to. Prince Harming had been the deal maker. And although I never negotiated terms or credit lines, I was responsible for every last dime.

I explained when they called, "Prince Harming emptied the bank account and left town." They didn't care. I understood. One of our clients had a wife who was very ill with MS and they had large medical bills. And no matter how much they pleaded there was nothing I could do. I had nothing to give.

I received another bid request for a clean out from Don in the beginning of June. I was more certain of the process and comfortable that Don and I were going to be able to work together. It was pretty straightforward. I was keeping it together. Barely.

If only the business had been my only issue.

One night at home, the downstairs toilet backed up. I called the plumber who had recently helped me with a sink problem. Cody, now 17, seemed to have forgotten we didn't have a disposal and stuffed corn down the drain.

The plumber was there about 45 minutes and informed me because the problem was on the house side of the curb, it was my responsibility to replace the plumbing from the road to the house. "Yah, see the roots from that tree have interrupted the flow and there's nothing else I can do. It's gonna cost ya," he said almost playfully.

I was in disbelief. He went on to say as long as we didn't use the downstairs bathroom, we should be okay for a little while. Not even a week later I was washing the dishes and water started dripping on my head. It was coming from the master bathroom. This was the charming home with the red cedar siding and the flowers planted in the front. Yes, this was my life.

There's a child's bible song that tells of the foolish man who built his house upon the sand. I was that foolish man. My life was built on lies and manipulation. Everything was crumbling.

I hadn't been able to make my mortgage since April. We were heading into July. I had come to terms with the fact I was completely underwater—but I had no idea how much.

One day I stayed in my pajamas, put my hair in a ponytail and dug up every invoice I could find. I had already started creating a list of the debtors that called me. There were so many. I was stunned by the numbers. Ignorant and naïve, I expected it would be maybe fifty thousand dollars of debt. But as I watched that number come and go, my heart was beating fast and I could feel panic closing in.

Horrified, I checked my addition again and again.

The numbers were staggering. I owed more than a half-million dollars.

Me, Teresa Martin, who not even three years ago owed less than two grand on my Honda Accord and had only one credit card with a two hundred and fifty dollar credit limit.

How? How could I be so fucking stupid? As much as I wanted to blame Prince Harming, once again, it all fell back on me.

I felt like God was on direct-connect. I talked to Him throughout the day. I didn't ask for help with specific things like more money. Just peace and strength. I prayed, *"Please God, just give me strength to stand through this and peace to get through the process."* I wanted to make it through this storm sober. Stronger.

Bea knocked on the door with her reliable, white, beaming smile. She was giving me a ride to meet with a bankruptcy attorney. I'm so glad I didn't have to do this by myself. I was advised to file bankruptcy for both businesses, the manufactured home dealer and construction company, along with personal bankruptcy. I had a five hundred thousand plus debt with no means to pay it back. This doesn't even take into consideration the taxes I hadn't filed for 2001 and 2002, which cannot be included in the bankruptcy.

I needed to make money to pay for the filing.

One day at time.

One step at a time.

Remember to breathe and don't drink.

"You need to just come camping with all of us," Bea said while driving back to my place. I know she meant well, but it was the last thing I felt like doing. I only wanted to curl up in a ball and cry myself to sleep until it was all over.

Maybe she was concerned if they left me alone I might get drunk. Who knows? Maybe I would have.

I didn't think so. There were plenty of hours by myself that if I'd really wanted to, I could have. I knew if I just kept making good decisions, did the best I could, I would move forward and someday this would all be in my past. I knew if I had any chance of restoring myself to the once-inspiring gal who accomplished so much in her 20s, I could only do it sober. That was my only chance.

But I agreed to go. We went to a big AA campout at Lake Billy Chinook. What a beautiful place. Under the starry night I could imagine a day, not too far away, that I would be free. Free to pursue life in a big way. Maybe get back into sales and start running again. It gave me a breather from reality long enough to dream and hope for more, someday.

Everybody that was anybody was there—the clique from Saturday morning and Sunday night meetings.

A few times, I heard people referring to Dan and Bea as the "King and Queen of AA"—kind of like how I once thought of them as "regal." But these comments were not said in a flattering way. I took note.

We had a great time and if I hadn't already wanted what Bea had, I now wanted to be her when I grew up. This woman had so much fun. She had a full life! She golfed, scuba dived, travelled, water skied, she even drove the boat. She didn't wait for a man to be able to do anything. When I was little we had a boat and my mom would never drive. In fact, my mom never even drove a car.

I loved Bea's verve.

She taught me how to water-ski that weekend. I got up pretty quick. As I was hanging out with a life preserver in the middle of that massive body of water, the great mysteries of the deep surrounding me, it resembled my life. I was wading around with intention to rise. I had many unanswered questions and not sure what lay ahead, but I trusted. Just like I trusted the life preserver to keep me afloat, I trusted

God would keep me lifted up. I would rise.

***

Don from Mutual Bank had sent me a few jobs over the last couple of months and Bea was my go-to gal on all of them. She loved having her "play" money and we worked well together. But with me filing bankruptcy we would no longer be able to accept the cleaning jobs. They were essentially contracts and needed to be bid out to a licensed business.

One day, Bea asked, "What would it take to get a cleaning business going? It would be great to keep working together."

I explained the process of getting the license, insurance and bank account. She needed to get Dan's blessing, but soon enough we were going into business together. The cleaning business was already established with tools, supplies and Don as our one and only client. The intention was the business would eventually be transferred back to me once I was back on my feet.

I felt excited and hopeful. An answer to my prayers.

***

I needed to have a conversation with my boys to tell them we were moving, again. We were going to lose the home, and all the cars. I had no idea what I would drive or even if I would drive. I had no idea where we were going to live or how I was going to provide for them. Austin still lived primarily at his dad's. But his dad had been much more flexible with my time with him and I saw him much more than the courts ordered. I still needed to make sure I paid his child support.

A few months ago, I'd gotten behind and was issued a bench warrant. I went to jail even though I was current at the time. I had a pattern of being late. I was only locked up for a few hours, but I had my mug shot taken and thumb printed. My attorney said, "Because you are a woman, the DA is making your case an example."

I bailed myself out of jail, but I still needed to stand in front of a judge for the charge. There was a slight possibility I could be sentenced to jail time. It wasn't probable, but possible. I didn't understand how politics works. My transgression seemed so minimal compared to people who were years behind—and they weren't going to jail. But if they could close my case with a compelling story that told voters, "We serve justice to the deadbeat parents that don't pay," the details didn't matter.

Just add this to the wreckage and devastation brought on by my choices.

One thing was certain, paying my child support superseded everything else.

I pray I haven't ruined my boys. I pray that I can and will do better in the future. There are no guarantees. God help me.

I called them into the room and told them, "I'm in way over my head with our home and finances. This means we will be moving and there could be other changes with the cars and stuff. I don't have a lot of answers right now, but I'll do my best to answer any questions you have."

Cody's eyes were wide and wondering. They were both such good boys. Cody was going into his final year of high school. His greatest love was basketball and when we moved to Oregon City at the end of 2000, he wasn't able to break into the team. The farmhouse came with a new high school and things didn't get any easier for him.

Now, another change was looming. I felt like a piece of shit. The truth was I screwed him over during his high school years. My numbing and avoiding with alcohol robbed him of the community he'd built — primarily with his basketball team. Cody was with that team for several years. When we lived in Seattle I drove him back to Portland for playoffs every weekend for months.

I couldn't change what had been done. I could only try to do better. It was almost unbearable to bring up. Not so much the conversation, but not having answers, landing us in a stillness with debris whirling around. And I was trying to reassure them everything was okay when we were not completely out of the storm.

'Where are we going to live?" asked Austin.

"I don't know just yet."

"Mom, you say you're so happy," said Cody, "but you're crying all the time..."

That was a hard one to explain. I started small, "I am free." And as if on cue the tears started to fall. "As long as I keep moving forward, I know everything is going to be alright. As long as I am sober I have the ability to make better choices. But it doesn't mean I won't have painful moments and get overwhelmed from time to time."

We talked about possibilities to come and then they simply shifted to what's for dinner.

It was a moment that didn't take a lot of time, but took all my energy.

Cody's observation was never far from my mind.

Especially when I talked with Candy.

A spicy-hot older woman in AA, with short, spiked black-changing-to-white hair, Candy reminded me of Tony Curtis. The mischievousness that played in his eyes also played in hers. She was super nice and had been in the program for a while. Bea was her sponsor, too.

"You're on the pink cloud," Candy told me one day. At first, I thought it just sounded nice. But as more people made the same comment, I got curious.

"What does being on a pink cloud mean?

Candy told me, "You're experiencing a temporary state of bliss that many newcomers go through.

Everything's great at first and you're real hopeful, like you are, but eventually you will come crashing into reality. It happens to most of us."

This made me nervous. What if I *was* on a pink cloud and I was going to crash, run out and drink myself numb. Who could blame me? That simply wasn't an option. I had come too far. I didn't need these thoughts in my head. *Temporary bliss.*

I never missed a meeting during this time. From March through September, I went to one, if not two, meetings every day. I did service work and greeted at the Sunday night meetings.

Remember that person who touched everyone as they walked through the door with a welcoming hug or handshake? That was me now. I opened and closed the noon meeting at the church most weekdays. Sometimes I was the only one there. Sometimes there would be just one other person who really needed someone, anyone, to listen.

Near the end of June I chaired the woman's Tuesday night meeting. I shared through tears and smiles my gratitude for the rooms of AA. For someone who spent her life not needing anyone, I was in such need right now.

After the meeting I sat on the church stoop with a couple gals. Micki had shoulder length brown hair, no makeup, and glasses. She was sharp with a sweet little family and a husband in AA. She reminded me of Velma from Scooby-Doo.

"Where are you going to live?" she asked.

"I'm not sure. I'm hoping to stay in town. This is where all my friends are and I like the meetings here."

"Steve's son is moving out of his condo on Territorial Road. I don't think he's rented it yet. Do you want me to ask him about it for you?"

"Yes, of course. That would be great!" Things just might fall into place.

"I'll let you know as soon as I talk to him."

A few days later I saw Micki again. She had mentioned it to Steve and he had said yes, but when she asked for a couple provisions, Steve said he needed to think about it. I never knew exactly what her requests were. I was nervous about asking for anything beyond a roof over our heads.

July 1. Hip hip hooray! We have a place to stay.

"As long as you take the home as is . . . ," Steve said, "I could rent it for a reduced price for the first six months and then we will revisit the rent amount."

I had no idea what "as is" meant. I went over about a week later to check out our new home. The kitchen wasn't much bigger than my then-bathroom, but it had a window, that opened! There was a pass-through that looked into the dining room/living room. The only natural light for the large room came through a sliding patio door at the end. There were two bedrooms and a bathroom with a washer and dryer in it. That was a bonus, as I had sold ours—to Micki, as a matter of fact.

The house was a disaster. His son had lived there with some roommates and it appears they had a lot of fun. The carpets were dark and beer-soaked. Food and garbage were everywhere. I would guess nothing had ever been cleaned during their stay at Condo de Steve. But this was nothing compared to some of the shit holes I had been cleaning out.

It was a place I could plant my son and me until I got on my feet. I'd have six months to do it.

Okay—done. This was perfect, for now. At least I could check off this major item from my to-do list.

Now for transportation. I tried to refinance one of my cars to get the payment down to something I might have a better chance of paying. They refused to work with me because my credit was dirt.

I tried to make them understand: "If you don't help me reduce this payment you're going to have to repossess it."

I was desperate.

And they did indeed repossess it a couple weeks later, but not before Les Schwab took their rims and tires back. It was humiliating. And then the service vehicles were repossessed. It was bound to happen after I'd missed several months' payments.

Repossession was tough. One creditor snuck in in the middle of the night and took appliances, ripped up the carpets, removed the chandelier from the dining room, and emptied the make-shift garage of anything of value. It was like being robbed. I know they were entitled and I owed them, but it still felt dirty and wrong.

I hadn't even reached the door when the neighbor girls told me that a few guys were there last night and took a bunch of stuff. I probably could have called the cops, but the truth was I didn't want to fight any longer. I wanted to get through this as quickly as possible.

It was traumatic and embarrassing, but, with each repossession, I felt like I was moving forward. I knew I couldn't keep these things. I didn't want them. I wanted to be as far away from this business and this life as possible. And the longer I went through the process of breaking down the old to get through it, the more I started regretting the decision to stay in that business with Bea. It felt like I was dragging the past along with me.

Next mountain, taxes. I met with another fellow AA'er, John. He told me to get all my receipts together and showed me how to categorize them. This was going to be a task. There were boxes and boxes of paperwork in a newly, yet typical, unfinished office space we made in a small shop building. None of it organized. Coupons and receipts were mixed in with bids and anything else imaginable.

This will take forever, I thought, but I couldn't get to

where I want to be without going through this.

I started sorting.

CHAPTER TEN

Love

The heart knows.

Every recovery professional says not to get in a serious relationship in your first year.

One day after the noon meeting my AA friend Tom came up behind me and wrapped his arms around me. It felt nice and warm, but uncomfortable, because I didn't think it was just a friendly hug.

Bea, my ever-playful sponsor, said, "I think he's interested in you."

"Yah, but I'm not interested in him. He's not my type."

Her eyes grew round and curious, "Oh yeah, what's your type?"

"I'm not even ready. I have so much to take care of before that could even happen," I paused.

"Besides, aren't you supposed to wait a year before starting a relationship or something like that?"

"There's nothing wrong with dating," she smiled. "Just don't get too serious."

"Victor. I would want someone like Victor. He's got a lot of sober time," I said. In truth, Victor mirrored what she had. She and Dan went hand-in-hand in program and they had a full and active life. "He is a doting dad, and seems calm and pleasant."

She didn't say anything after that. I felt embarrassed.

A couple days went by and while we were at her house planning a job, I awkwardly brought up our conversation: "I'm embarrassed by my admission about Victor."

She dismissed it with a wave of her hand and said, "If you would pick Victor at least I know your picker is not broken."

We both laughed and I thought that was the end of it. But when we were getting ready to go camping a week later, she mentioned that Victor would be there.

"You're evil," I said.

"Yes, I am."

The camping trip was uneventful in terms of Victor and me. But there were a few moments I scratched my head in puzzlement. Bea got pissy about Victor when he went off with his daughter and didn't really socialize with the group.

"I don't know why he even came up here if he wasn't going to hang out with us. He should have just gone camping on his own!" she spat.

I had never seen this side of Bea. It wasn't charming. Was it because she was trying to play matchmaker? I hoped not. That would have been even more embarrassing.

Dan had a constant companion that weekend. I'd seen Rich a few times before. He was the one Prince Harming gave his AA card to that Sunday night. He was also the same lost little boy with the ringlets who sat between Dan and Bea at my first meeting a few months ago. He seemed nice enough.

"He's in a complicated marriage with a much older woman. There isn't any love between them. It's more a marriage of convenience. She doesn't get in the way of his going out and drinking and he takes care of the bills," Bea shared. "They've been off and on for years."

He had a tattoo: "Rich Loves Lisa." I assumed that was his wife's name. It seemed like an awful big commitment for a marriage of convenience and with no love in the game.

We all went to a cove where a rope swing hung. Everybody took a turn except for me and Bea. We watched and cheered. Rich took a turn and let go a bit too soon. He landed badly. When he stood up all color had drained from his face. His eyes were wide open and his jaw was clenched. Not everybody had noticed what had happened. I winced as I watched him try to move without moving too much. As he stepped aside I could see the jagged rock he'd just hit full force. He was in so much pain and I felt bad for him. Later, he wasn't shy about sharing the nasty black bruise that spread over the top of the crack of his ass. It was a direct hit to his tailbone.

A week or two later Bea called and said, "Rich is riding with us to the speaker meeting."

I thought it was weird that he was going with us and that she thought it was necessary to tell me. But we all headed off together to a large speaker meeting in the northwest part of the city.

What I learned that evening was Rich was quiet and he was a hard worker. He had struggled with alcohol most of his adult life. He was referred to as a retread: someone who routinely goes to AA, gets a little time sober and then goes back out drinking.

The word re-tread seemed so insensitive, but there

was a mix of contradictions in the rooms I hadn't quite understood. Like, being rigorously honest. According to Bea, there were shades of truth.

Or that recommendation that you shouldn't get in a relationship for at least one year. Although I wasn't in a romantic relationship, I had just entered a business relationship with my sponsor. I was also surprised how many long-term sobers would romantically pursue newbies.

I sensed an innocence about Rich. He was quiet, but when he did speak he seemed honest in a childlike way. When a child speaks they don't think about how their words might be interpreted. They speak a raw, unedited truth. That's how Rich spoke. But I wasn't confident in my intuition, yet. Even though Bea said she thought my picker wasn't broken, the sprawling wasteland of my past indicated a much different truth, Prince Harming, Tory, Rex, Ricky…

Since I'd seen him at my first meeting, Rich seemed to come in and out of AA every few weeks. I found it interesting the amount of grace they extended Rich for his in and out approach. There was a gal who was trying hard to work her program and they were indifferent —almost dismissive—about her efforts.

"Looks like Maria is trying real hard," I would suggest, not knowing any better.

"Yeah, we'll see," Bea would say with an eye roll and a shrug. Almost like, yep, here she goes again-- expecting her to fail.

I didn't get it.

I wondered where the grace started and ended.

Why were some drunks given immunity for their slips and others weren't?

I was under the impression that we were all broken and it took as long as it took to get sober. Our leaders were servants, not governors, and the only requirement for membership was the desire to quit drinking.

Who determined when someone was a wasted cause?

And what if I drank again? Would they open their arms or would I be shunned and talked about like Maria?

I was realizing that part of being sober was no longer being able to ignore red flags and my intuition.

It was beginning to feel a little reminiscent of my Bell Rose experience as a young girl. "While the church people would say "Love one another," they'd whisper and gossip about each other.

After Sunday night meetings, we'd head to the ice cream shop or local burger hut for a sweet treat. I didn't partake in the sweets, but enjoyed the conversation. I had started Atkins about six weeks before and was already down twenty-five pounds with my low-carb diet and my running. Most of our clique was doing some variation of Atkins.

I was starting to feel better about my health and my body. I still had a long way to go, but it wasn't my primary focus.

One night, I was getting ready to leave and Bea followed me out. She said they didn't have room for Austin and me in their car and were going to ask Rich to bring us to the next camping trip.

I smelled a rat. But she was my sponsor and would never do anything to jeopardize my program. Would she?

If they wanted me to ride up with Rich, I would. It had to be on the up and up. He was married, loveless or not, and my life was still so unsettled. Certainly, there was no hidden agenda, right?

Besides, I was more interested in learning to get up on one waterski and teach Austin what I'd learned than in developing a romance.

Rich showed up late Friday afternoon. He helped load our things in the back of his pickup. I was wearing shorts and a tank top and had my hair in two braids.

"Your braids are cute," he said. I was shocked that he spoke and that he gave me a compliment. It was sweet.

He had a Ford Lightning pickup and I wondered how comfortable being stuffed in the middle of the two-seater would be. I was about to find out.

Rich attempted to chat with Austin.

"How's your summer going?" he asked.

"Good." Austin replied.

"Have you ever been camping?"

"Not really."

"Are you excited about it?"

"I guess."

Crickets.

I could feel a weird nervousness in him.

Why would he be nervous? Was this a setup? Was he in on it?

The AA gang had told me he probably wouldn't talk much. But he chatted non-stop from the time we left the city all the way to the campsite. It was over a three-hour drive. "Is Lisa your wife?" I interjected at one point.

"What?"

"The name in your tattoo…It says Rich loves Lisa."

"Oh. No, that was my ex," he explained. "She lives in Georgia with my son."

"Oh?"

"I found out she was cheating on me and I couldn't take it. I tried. I tried staying in a small apartment above the shop I worked at. But one day, I said fuck it. I threw my stuff in the back of my truck and drove to my grandma's in Canby."

He paused like he was reliving it.

"I had to stop one time in Wyoming. Just for a few hours, because the snow was so bad. I chugged down a six-pack, slept a couple hours, and got back at it. I didn't stop until I got there."

I could tell this caused him a lot of pain. It happened a few years ago, but the way his face changed and the way his words landed, it still felt raw. I guessed he had not yet healed from this.

Somewhere about two hours into the ride I stopped thinking about ulterior motives and just listened to his stories. I thought it was odd how this man was in a marriage, but seemed so absolutely alone. Everything was "I," not "we." But it wasn't like he was consciously omitting the wife; he really identified as being alone.

How sad, I thought.

Could I marry a man with another woman's name tattooed on his chest?

We arrived at the campsite, where Austin and I were sharing a tent with Candy. She was very interested in what was happening with me and Rich. "You know Rich's wife is my age," she said as we got ready for bed.

I said, "Yeah, I heard something like that."

"It's nice to know age doesn't matter. I hear he's ending the marriage," she said with a wink and a smile.

Her smile reminded me of the Cheshire Cat's smile in Alice in Wonderland, big and mischievous. I was waiting for a big tongue to roll out and lick her chops.

"Whatever, Candy," I giggled. Thank goodness it was getting dark because I felt my face burning. I was surprised that I felt protective of Rich. He didn't need a barracuda launching an attack if he was trying to get out of a bad marriage. I might have been a little jealous, too.

I'd made a habit of thanking God for my blessings every night in my journal. Tonight would be no different.

"And, God, please help me not have feelings for this guy," I wrote.

After two days of waterskiing and swimming and

hanging out on the beach, we loaded up the truck and headed home.

We drove in comfortable silence. The road took us high above lush green valleys and just below tree-covered mountaintops through the Mount Hood National Forest.

The sun sank low in the sky. I looked over at Rich and, for a moment, time stopped. I could see forever in his eyes. Past the beautiful amber-green color. I went deeper.

There the oddest question came into my mind: "Would you care for this man if he was unable to care for himself?"

What? But I knew in the depth of my soul I would. And I answered, "Yes." I felt like spirit had lifted me to another place and time to have this conversation.

I wasn't sure what this meant. But I knew I cared deeply for this man and I would never hurt him.

There were so many obstacles for both of us. Love was the last thing I needed in my life right now. At least the kind of love I had always known that came at great costs and consequences. And he was married!

I returned in the middle of Rich telling a story, "Yah, when I was, I don't know 12 maybe 13, I used to ride my bike for miles. I would ride it from Canby to Molalla to hang out with friends. You know that big hill down Ivy Street? I never batted an eye about going up that on my bike when I was younger…"

The energy was calm. We were all pretty mellow and the drive created a nice transition from fun in the sun to welcome home.

He helped unload our stuff.

I wanted to hug him and say, "Take care of yourself. Please don't drink. And I hope to see you soon."

Instead I said, "Thanks for everything." And that was it.

Over the next couple of weeks, we saw each other at meetings, and Dan and Bea invited us both to other speaker meetings and a movie. We could have shut it down at any time, but we really enjoyed talking with each other. He'd sit on my front porch and eat McDonald's after work. We'd talk for a few hours and then he would go home.

While it wasn't physical, we were connecting. One night when he was getting ready to leave, we both could feel the impending kiss, but consciously withdrew.

I told him as long as he was still with his wife, nothing could ever happen. Not even a kiss.

I didn't see him for a few days. That was understandable. He had only been sober for ninety days, this time.

Did I hear myself?! He was only sober ninety days. And I was only forty-five days ahead of him! Not to mention my life was in ruins. I had no business getting involved with this guy. What was I thinking? What were Dan and Bea thinking?

One night in the end of July, Rich stopped by with his hamburger bag in hand. This guy eats way too much McDonalds, I thought.

I came out on the front porch, as usual. He was quiet. We just sat there until he was getting ready to leave. I was certain he had come to say it wasn't going to work out. He wasn't going to leave his wife.

As if he could read my mind, he said, "I'm going to

talk to her this week…I'm going to leave."

I didn't say anything at first. I just let that land.

"You're not doing this because of me, are you?" I asked.

"No." he said. "We've never been like husband and wife. I have been putting this off thinking maybe my drinking is why I was so unhappy, but my life is why I was so unhappy."

That made a lot of sense to me. I got it.

***

I focused on our move. Cody and I packed up the house.

This move was really going to be our fresh start. I was leaving the house where my life was nearly destroyed. But it was also the house where my soul reached out for help. Where my spirit was set free to lead. Where I dropped to my knees, took the hand of Jesus and surrendered.

I hadn't even lived in this old farmhouse for an entire year and I was so glad to be going. In this dark, gloomy, oppressive house, I was set free. A real juxtaposition.

It was late. I was up in my bedroom. The windows were open on both sides and the wind blew the sheers into the room and sucked them out on the other side. The bedside lamp filled the room with a soft glow as Three's Company came on. I watched old sitcom reruns to help me unwind to fall asleep. The phone rang.

"I moved out." Rich said, "I'm staying with Dan and Bea for now. I'm unpacking and I'll call you tomorrow."

It was matter of fact. Just like that. I didn't know what this really meant. I was confused and not sure if I was ready to get involved. Was my picker any good? I felt excited that he was taking the steps for us to have a chance. Maybe I would have my happily ever after? I got back up and started packing. I needed to be physical to process my thoughts.

That Saturday morning, I stood near the meeting entrance. "All the guys went skiing this morning," Bea told me when she came strolling by.

"Oh?" I responded, pretending I didn't care or I wasn't sure why she was telling me. But I did care and I was sure. I was crazy curious to know what was going on with Rich.

Candy walked in to the meeting. I wonder if she heard that Rich left his wife? Oh, I hated this. I hated feelings of jealousy. I just wanted to know what HE was thinking.

The meeting was getting ready to start. There was an open chair next to me at the opposite end of the room from the door. When Rich came in, he bee-lined towards me in the corner, nearly tripping over his own feet. Funny, awkward, child-like. I was mesmerized.

We sat through the meeting not saying anything to each other. At the end he walked me out and said he would see me tonight. He had some things he had to take care of.

Well, that answered a lot of questions. Not!

Why was I feeling so nervous? Why was I letting this take up so much space in my mind? I felt like I was going crazy. I had REAL problems to deal with: Money, taxes, job, business, child support, just to name a few.

It was getting dark when he knocked on the door. I opened it and stood aside, inviting him in. This was the first time he had ever been in my home. We always kept his visits on the front porch. Boxes and packing materials were everywhere, but I had a pot roast in the oven. I always cooked. I rarely ate McDonalds.

I wondered if he was hungry. He didn't have his hamburger bag with him this time.

Daisy, my easy-going little Shih Tzu who rarely barked, yapped and yapped as Rich stepped in. That got my attention. I peered at him side-eyed to see what was up.

Please, Spirit, reveal to me if this man is no good, I prayed.

I motioned him to the couch while I checked on dinner. Soon Daisy was up in his lap and checking him out. Her front paws rested on his chest, hind legs staggering on each of his legs and her tail straight and wagging swiftly. Her nose sniffed his face. Like she was giving him the run-down.

We sat on the couch and he told me everything. How he and his wife had gotten together. She worked at a tavern and served him free beer.

At the time, he felt nearly destroyed by his son's mother's affair and had driven across the country in record time to try to escape the agony. They'd been together for nearly a decade. Alcohol was the only thing that could manage his pain.

During the course of his current marriage he was not always faithful. He suspected she wasn't either, but he didn't care. He didn't try to make himself look innocent and assured me that it was over. It had been over for years. He had been just too tired and lazy to do anything about it. It had been easier to stay and she didn't get in the way of his drinking.

I knew that feeling all too well. Unfortunately, I witnessed this my entire life with my mom and then me. Too hard to make a change. Easier to stay.

Plus, our sponsors had brought us together and that, I assumed, meant we had their blessing. They were my guides. They knew what was best. At just over four months sober, who was I to know any different?

While Daisy snored on the floor just a few feet away, the roast cooled on the counter and the TV played in the background, Rich leaned in and we kissed.

As we lay on the couch watching TV, he asked me, "Will we always lay together like this?"

"We can if we want to," I said.

We both agreed to take it slow and I escorted him to the door. We kissed goodnight. And I hugged him close. I closed the door.

Can this really be happening? I am so happy.

Oh my God, I'm so insane.

CHAPTER ELEVEN

LETTING GO

To thine own self be true.

Hamlet, William Shakespeare

"Never be bullied into silence. Never allow yourself to be made a victim. Accept no one's definition of your life, but define yourself."

— Harvey Fierstein

August 2003

Red and blue lights swirled and flashed while a large chirp got my attention. It was the final and fifteenth load moving to the condo and I just wanted it done. I'd borrowed a truck from Cody's dad, Ricky. The small bed made the task much tougher than a U-Haul, but it was free and got the job done.

"License and registration, please," asked the officer.

I didn't ask why. I handed it over.

"Do you know why I pulled you over?"

"Yes, sir, I was speeding." I couldn't look him in the eye. I had never had a father confront me when I'd screwed up, but I could imagine it would stir a similar feeling of shame.

"Alright, stay put. I'll be right back." He walked at a snail's pace back to his car. It was a hot August day and I was filthy with dirt and sweat from head to toe. When he came back he handed me a ticket and told me, "Have a nice day."

Why do they say that? Have a nice day! Right! Pay one hundred and twenty-five dollars, have a nice day!

My old self might have gone down the rabbit hole of blame, failure and "why me??" But I simply folded the ticket up, put it in my wallet and carried on. I was closing a chapter of pain and hopelessness. I was excited about my new beginning and this little bump in the road wasn't going to slow me down. I was ready for my fresh start in the condo.

Because of the bankruptcies, I didn't have to worry about all that was wrong with the farmhouse: the plumbing, carpenter ants, slugs that ruled the back deck, diseased trees, sinking pier block foundation, old creditors coming through and pillaging whatever they liked. Nor did I need to fear Prince Harming knowing where I was. Nope, not any longer.

I was free.

Well, freer.

Don't get me wrong. Bankruptcy is not exactly a desired destination. It's not a financial plan I recommend, and not only because you don't have any spending cash.

I just had no choice. I am still dumbfounded that I could go from two thousand to over five hundred thousand dollars of debt in just over two years. It was stupefying, but it was like earning a PhD in Life…

I learned how I limited myself. Prince Harming was able to ask for things I would have never been bold enough to ask for. I never thought myself worthy of that type of credit. As it turns out I wasn't. But I would never even have asked.

I also learned that having a lot of money didn't make my life better. I craved simplicity, quiet and safety. Like that woman I'd envied playing with her child on the lawn last summer. I learned what really mattered.

***

My tax debt hadn't been revealed yet, but once it was complete, no matter how bad, it would be the starting point. That's when all the anxious guessing would end and I would know where I stood. Then I could plot, plan, and build from there.

As it was, I was barely making it. Jobs from Don were few and far between. I'd had to apply for food stamps. That was difficult. Being independent was so important to me.

And almost as if perfectly orchestrated, I'd repeated the legacy of the women in my family. What I fought so hard to prevent, I unconsciously re-created with the choices I made. In less than a decade, my life repeated all the dependence, domestic abuse, adultery, and alcohol abuse I'd learned.

Business had nearly dried up. Bea and I placed an ad for commercial cleaning in a local newspaper—always an effective marketing tool when I had the construction business. We didn't get one call from the ads. Cold calls weren't panning out, either. We had known that we would need to build the business, but had no idea it would be so difficult. Prince Harming made it look so simple. He had the right angle at the right time for the right industry, I suppose.

Or maybe my heart just wasn't in it.

Because the checks went to Bea, I had to ask her for money. It was so uncomfortable. I knew it needed to be this way, but I was spending so many hours doing a job I hated, and I couldn't even cover my bills. Dan and Bea showed me the profit and loss statements — pointing out how the company wasn't making enough money.

This business felt like it was just stretching out the pain and struggle that had become the wreckage of

Prince Harming. It was an extension of the life I wanted so desperately to move on from.

I never doubted Dan and Bea's integrity or how they were running the finances.

Even though I was working hard, there just wasn't enough work and therefore not enough money.

I knew I could cover the rent and child support for September. But I also knew the work orders were going to get even fewer with winter coming in. I had enough going on that I just figured we'd worry about it then.

While once we talked a few times a day, Bea and I now talked only when we had to. I initially thought it was because I just wasn't as available for chatting because I was now involved with Rich. But I had come to understand there was something else brewing.

When I wasn't stressing about the business, I spent my time hanging out with Rich. He and Cody got along really well, when Cody was home. He had found a new love interest and spent a lot of his time with her. Austin liked Rich's choice of music, hard rock, and his cool, fast truck. And Rich's video gaming had them both dialed in as friends. It was all pretty easygoing. Nothing pretentious, no acting on good behavior. I guess that could be a benefit of meeting in AA: your baggage is put out on display. Take it or leave it.

One afternoon, I heard Bea knocking at the door. She was pissed that she'd just gotten a speeding ticket. "How dare he hide? It's just not right that it changes speeds that drastically right there!" she fumed. And on she ranted into her phone to Dan as she walked through the door.

She had come to bring me a check I had requested to help me with rent. She hung up the phone and told me what had happened. I just listened. I had received that ticket just a couple months ago. I was speeding and I accepted it. To me, it was that rigorous honesty thing. If I hadn't been speeding, I wouldn't have got the ticket. Seemed simple.

She wouldn't let it go.

This was similar to the same incensed behavior I witnessed when Victor didn't join in the group activities at Lake Billy Chinook.

She finally changed the subject, saying, "Your place

is coming together nicely."

I looked around at what I had accomplished and said, "Thanks."

And then we started talking about Rich and me.

"If Victor was to become available and interested in you would that change your feelings for Rich?" she asked.

I was shocked. I thought we had her blessing and this is what she and Dan wanted.

"No. I love Rich."

"You know Rich brought his wife on our boat and hung out with us."

What the hell? I'm grasping for some line of reason here. What's the point of her saying all this?

"Why are you bringing this up now?" I asked.

"I thought you should know."

"Know what?" I asked.

"That things may not have been as bad as you thought." Her phone rang. The conversation was over and she headed out the door.

Wow! What just happened here? Why was she doing this? And is it true? Had Rich been happily married?

But that's not what everybody had told me. Not just Dan and Bea, but even members from Al-Anon that met downstairs during our meetings had said the same thing.

I *have to ask Rich about this. And what's he going to say? Would he say, "Yes, yes, we were fine, and when I met you I couldn't live without you?" What have I done?*

I felt the old, powerless spinning in my mind again.

When I asked Rich about it he seemed indifferent: "Yeah, she went with us once. But it wasn't any big deal. And it was only once."

He was as perplexed as I was about why Bea would bring this up now. I asked him again, "Am I the reason you left your wife?" He said, "No, but..."

"But what?" I asked.

"But I probably wouldn't have been so determined and done it so fast."

Well, what does a girl do with that?

I sat on it.

A few days later, on our way to do a Mutual Bank job for Don, I broached a conversation with Bea.

I knew I had to do something different to provide for me and my boys. I just had to make money.

"I would like to go back into professional sales, wear a suit again, and have business meetings," I said. I described how I wanted to pick up where I'd gone off course.

"I was really good at sales and it paid well," I added.

"Well, not everybody gets to do what they want," she snapped. "Not everybody gets to dress up and go to work."

It wasn't just her words--it was also the ugly sneer and her tone that hurt me. She was pissed. Why wouldn't she want me to do better if I could?

It was similar to the day she got her ticket.

She seemed offended that I would even suggest doing something other than cleaning houses.

We got into the house and went about our business. We didn't say a word to each other. I was crushed that my hero was mad at me.

And then a familiar feeling started coming over me. I couldn't identify it immediately, but it felt like gloom. No, I felt trapped. Eerily, much like I had with Prince Harming, I thought: This is too complicated to change so I'll just have to suffer and live with my choices.

Bea dropped me off and, clearly still annoyed, barely said goodbye.

I didn't feel I had her support to pursue other employment options. We were in a business relationship together and that would remain the priority.

So I started looking for part-time jobs to supplement my income. I applied for a full-time position at the local police station— sheepish, feeling like a criminal. I still had some self-identification issues. They never called.

The local health club hired me, though. It didn't pay much, but it was something. And I really loved being in the health and wellness industry. Helping people to become better.

I remembered just before getting involved with my

mentor and ex-boss, Tory, I had begun growing professionally and personally. My life had been on an upswing. I was proud of who I was becoming. I ran most mornings, sometimes at lunch. Even after a few drinks in the evening, I would run around the lake when I lived in Lake Oswego. I rode trails on my Trek mountain bike. I hiked and I walked for miles. Cody and I roller bladed the waterfront boardwalk. I missed that part of my life and wanted to bring it back.

So, I began walking and running regularly. I had lost about 40 pounds total and all the activity and endorphins helped me manage my panic and anxiety. It was a tool I relied on a lot during this time—burning off all the extra energy so it didn't land in my mind. I also felt closer to God when I was out on the road and in nature.

"It's not good to run so much," Bea warned me. "You better not to over-do it."

I listened to what she was saying, but paid no mind to it. I was free. I could run again. I could choose for myself again. Not just going through the motions to meet others' needs and my had-to's. I had to gather my receipts. I had to find a home. I had to find a way to feed my kiddo's. I had to find a way to pay child support.

I had to do all those things, but I GOT to run. One of the first feelings of returning to myself.

I was beginning to take charge. It was small, but it mattered.

***

The day to face the judge about my child support in arrears was upon me. I was nervous. I hadn't been late for almost a year, but who knew what the District Attorney's plan was, particularly if they were indeed using me as an example. I dressed respectfully in a skirt and top. My sister stood by my side.

The judge entered and I started shaking. *What if he orders me to jail?* My sister held my hand. He called me forward and asked the DA, "Has Ms. Martin been timely with her payments?"

"Yes, your Honor, for the past eleven months Ms. Martin has made all her payments as scheduled."

He asked, "What do you recommend?"

My breath stopped.

"Our office recommends she attends and completes

court-ordered parenting classes and probation for the time period of at least 24 months."

The judge turned to my attorney, "Do you have anything to add?"

"No, your Honor," he responded.

Looking at me, the judge said, "Young lady, you have a responsibility to your child. You do what you're supposed to do and I won't see you back in here." He turned to the court. "I agree with the DA, Ms. Martin is to attend and complete parenting classes and will receive 24 months of probation. If she stays current with her financial obligation to her child support as scheduled for the 24-month period, the case will be closed."

I was dismissed. Later, I learned I had to pay for these parenting classes. But I was free. God, help me. I was free.

I was checking things off my list and moving forward.

I felt optimistic. Maybe my life was finally going to be OK. Maybe I would stay on my pink cloud. *Maybe.*

Little did I know, disaster lurked around the corner.

Our jobs from Mutual Bank had dwindled. I emailed Bea and asked for our bank balance.

 "There is no money," she replied. "We need to get some work orders."

"I don't know what else we can do," I said.

I was worried.

She contacted Don at Mutual Bank in Seattle and arranged a meeting without consulting me about my availability. She scheduled it for a day I had Austin.

"Bea, I have Austin that day."

She made no apology.

"I can drive and pick you up around 8am," she said. The business was her priority.

Why was she taking this stance? This was play money for her and the intention was to turn the business over to me at some point. This was cruel. She more than anybody knew my struggles with my ex. None of this felt good.

Fortunately, Austin's dad changed days and I was able to make the meeting.

The trip up was silent and uncomfortable. Resentful and worried, I started to shut down. We took Don to lunch and he was very pleasant. A little heavier, with dark hair, and a gentle face, he reminded me of one of my uncles.

He told us that it wasn't that he didn't want to give us work, but the department was being reorganized and there wasn't any work to be issued. I knew what that meant and I knew what was coming.

It would only be a matter of time until their manufactured home department would suffer the same fate as my other client that went bankrupt, owing me over eighty thousand dollars. When we got back in the car to ride home, we chatted about how nice Don was and how well the meeting went.

I voiced my concerns about the future of our one billable client.

Bea didn't want to hear it. "If you don't want to clean homes, I'll clean them myself!" she snapped.

The truth is I didn't want to clean homes. I wanted a real job I could count on. I wanted to start fresh. I should have never agreed to go into business. Not then. Not with my sponsor. And not with me. I was way too screwed up to build a new business. It was crazy to be starting a company while filing bankruptcy for two failing businesses. I fucked up. In the past three months the business had brought in just twenty-three hundred dollars. And there was no work in the pipeline.

I had court-ordered parenting classes to pay for and child support coming due. Those were my priority. That meant rent was going to have to be late. I felt bad, but I didn't have any choice. If I didn't pay these two items, I would go to jail. It was that simple. I wasn't spending money frivolously; I had no money to do that. Rent would be late.

What I couldn't have imagined was my being late with rent becoming the hot topic of our AA community.

At Bea and Dan's annual Christmas party a few weeks later, several people came up to me and asked, "Are you okay?"

"I'm okay. Why do you ask?"

"I heard you're having some hard times."

"I'm going through some things," I said.

"Well, if your ass is on fire, get yourself to a meeting."

I felt like I was the talk of the town, but had no idea what exactly they were saying. I heard the whispers and saw the side glances. I couldn't have felt more uncomfortable in the very home where I had felt more connected to a woman, Bea, than I ever had in my life. The very home where we got on our knees and prayed together and I completed my fourth step. She was my mentor, my sponsor, my hero. I aspired to be like her.

How things had changed. At meetings Bea gave me the cold shoulder. I started looking for fulltime work.

Micki, the one who'd steered me to Steve's condo, reached out. I told her what was happening. I needed a job. I couldn't afford to live off the business. Bea wasn't talking to me anymore.

"Are you working your program?" Micki asked.

"My program? You mean the one where I turn to my sponsor if I think I'm going to drink? The one where I need to go to meetings if I'm having a rough time? Where everybody not only knows my name, but also knows my business?" I replied. I didn't want to take it out on Micki, but I was frustrated.

"What kind of program is this?" I went on.

"Well, what's going on with rent?"

"Our business isn't working. There are no work orders and no money in the bank. I put off looking for fulltime work because Bea went through the process of getting us set up for business. But it's just not working," I explained.

"You know Bea isn't your program."

"Well, it sure feels like it."

We talked a little while longer and I asked her if she would fill in as my sponsor. I couldn't call Bea and I wasn't sure if I would suddenly get hit with a desperate desire to drink. There was a definite conflict of interest with our work scenario. Funny. How could I have not predicted this back in July?

Micki agreed to be my sponsor.

In those intense months, I thought a lot about AA.

I didn't feel like my program was my priority anymore. And if I was really honest, I was beginning to think the "program" was a bunch of bullshit. I felt like finding a way to make a living and support myself and children should have been my priority. I had heard them say in meetings your program comes before anything. And I think that's just flat out wrong.

Or maybe me getting a job and taking care of business should have been my "program."

I decided right then to pull out from the business. I sent Dan and Bea an email and told them there was no way I could continue with it. They sent me a final profit and loss sheet along with a copy of everything Bea was entitled to. There was nothing left for me. It was painful on every level to walk away, but if I wanted to stay sober and have any chance at a full life, I had to do this.

And that was it. The end of my business relationship with my sponsor. I didn't pay October's rent until late October.

I stopped going to so many meetings. I was humiliated that people knew my failures and hated being ostracized.

But the good news was, I didn't feel like drinking either.

My focus was on doing better.

I went on a few interviews with manufactured home dealerships and they were excited to offer me a position, but I couldn't bring myself to stay in that industry. Each time I walked into a manufactured home, I experienced Prince Harming's reign all over again.

I started processing loan applications at home for a private mortgage broker and this helped, but it wasn't stable and didn't pay enough to rely on.

Then I read about a new weight loss company that was coming into the area and hiring counselors. I sent off my resume immediately for what felt like my dream job. I was so excited. This would be perfect.

Rich and I were working on our relationship. He had started staying with me and if it wasn't for his help, even though rent was late, it would not have been paid. He had accepted a position with an old employer in the Salem area. The commute was longer than he wanted, but he was working fulltime and seemed happy. He liked his general manager, Bennie, and wanted to do right by him. He felt like Bennie could see something in him that he was never able to see. I liked that he looked up to this man. It was good that he had someone whom he respected and honored as a role model.

While we had a nice easy flow to our relationship, I still had moments of insecurity. But I decided from the beginning I wasn't going to make him pay for my past. I was going to love him openly and honestly. If I hurt, I would tell him I hurt and not get angry and pissed off. If I was angry, I would tell him what I was angry about. He wasn't always perfect and neither was I. He could be super self-centered and for the most part I didn't mind, but there were times it would feel insensitive and selfish. We talked things through and didn't make each other play guessing games about what we were thinking or feeling.

A few days after I sent off the resume to the weight loss clinic, I got the call: "We'd like to meet with you about a position with our company."

I was over the moon. I would get to help people feel better. Could this really be true?

A picture floats around social media of Jesus holding a big teddy bear behind his back. "Trust me," he says to a little girl with a small teddy bear behind her back. "But God, I love it," she says. She doesn't want to let go of what she knows for sure.

I felt like that little girl. Bit by bit, I had to let go of the life I had, all that felt familiar, in order to receive what God had for me.

A bigger, fuller, richer life.

CHAPTER TWELVE

FREEDOM

"When I talk to addicted people, whether they are addicted to alcohol, drugs, gambling, Internet use, sex, or anything else, I encounter human beings who really do not have a viable social or cultural life. They use their addictions as a way of coping with their dislocation: as an escape, a pain killer, or a kind of substitute for a full life." [6]

–Bruce J. Alexander

[6] http://www.brucekalexander.com/articles-speeches/rat-park/148-addiction-the-view-from-rat-park

DECEMBER 2003

"You're hired!"

I had never heard more wonderful words. I was going back into a professional sales environment in an industry I had waded in, but never jumped into. They assigned me to a new weight loss clinic in Keizer, just outside Salem. It was quite a coincidence that Rich had just started working in Salem. If you believe in coincidences.

But I had no one in my AA community to celebrate with. My meeting attendance had fizzled to maybe once a week and, when I did go, it felt uncomfortable. Maybe it was my guilty conscience for bailing on a business I couldn't grow. Maybe it was my shame in starting something I couldn't finish. Or maybe it was the embarrassment that I failed, again—at business, at being a sponsee and a friend.

My sponsor no longer talked to me. For a while I knew there would always be a seat held for me next to Bea at the meetings. It symbolized my belonging and acceptance. The seat she once held for me now was always taken. The people in the rooms who still talked to me told me I was in danger of getting drunk again. Was it because I was shunned by my sponsor or because I wasn't going to as many meetings?

I began to worry.

Micki had agreed to be my sponsor, but we really didn't talk. No fault of hers. We were both busy. And twelve steps? What steps? I stopped at four.

Am I going to get drunk again? If I stay here and keep rehashing everything I've done wrong, I will.

Rich agreed to move down the freeway closer to where we both worked. Now eighteen, Cody was involved with a gal in Clackamas and decided to move in that direction.

So here we were in a brand-new city. We didn't know anyone or where anything was. Our first order of business was finding an AA meeting. We knew if we didn't get in a meeting we might both lose our sobriety.

I didn't know which of us was at greater risk: Rich the retread, or me, first-time sober. We got our handy little AA schedule and checked out a few meetings.

At a Saturday night meeting, the stories were the same as ones I'd heard before, only told by different people. It was a well-attended meeting with a raffle at the end. The older gentleman next to me won an elephant sitting on its back legs, covered in a patchwork of animal print. He handed it to me and said, "Here you go little lady. Enjoy it." It still sits in the entryway of my home to remind me of unexpected kindness in the world. But that night didn't work for our schedule and we didn't return to that meeting.

We tried another meeting that was held in a crowded halfway house. Add in some Doors music and bong hits, and it would have felt like a hippie party from the seventies. With people coming and going, it was terribly distracting. Neither of us could stay focused or follow who was speaking.

One of the last meetings we attended was in the back of a big church. It started off with the twelve steps and twelve traditions. The woman chairing the meeting was a bigger gal with long dark hair. She was loud, almost shouting. It became more like a sermon and I had flashbacks to the hell and damnation of the Bell Rose when I was a little girl.

I can giggle now. Each time we tried to resuscitate our program, we got redirected. We simply couldn't get dialed in. We couldn't find our home meeting, let alone one that felt just right.

None of these meetings were horrible, but our prior experience had tainted our expectation of what a meeting should be. That Sunday night clique was unique.

I saw that my program had been more about my relationship with my sponsor and our friendship. It was never really about "program"—not once had she asked me what step I was on or how were my steps going after the fourth.

My AA experience was different than most. It was more of a social club that turned into the school of hard knocks. It was never about drinking or not drinking for me. I never "needed" a meeting because I was going to drink. I looked forward to the meetings to see the people I had become fond of...the people I loved. When it was good, it was great. I felt loved and cared for, at first. It was what I needed at the time.

As I was maturing in my sobriety, I began to learn about the importance of understanding my needs and wants. And I learned what was important to me, not to Bea, or Prince Harming, or Tory...

When I left AA I realized sobriety was way more than not drinking. How long I didn't drink wasn't the issue— it was about how I lived my life. With a clear mind I was in charge of choices and able to listen to spirit for guidance. I was able to honor my values, ideals and needs. I had to live life as a whole-woman. Not just focus on drinking or not drinking. I realized if I wasn't true to me, I was sooner or later going to get drunk.

I began living wholly sober.

Both Rich and I worked on commission so we put in long hours. And we were happy. We were building our life together. We had very little when we first started out. And when we were able to shop to furnish our home together, my life felt normal, if there is such a thing, for the first time ever. Our lives were productive and purposeful.

Everything was clear and clean. We were together because we wanted to be together. There was no manipulation. No lies. No hidden agendas. Just us being real.

One of our favorite past-times was driving the countryside and scoping out new areas. We daydreamed of buying a home of our own someday. We talked about a shop for Rich so he could do side work. I imagined my big kitchen and the family gatherings we'd host. We both had dreams we could and did envision each other in.

We stopped trying to find a meeting in Salem and, one night, drove to our old Sunday night meeting. It felt weird walking into that old familiar church. Cold. A few people came up and were cordial. But we were definitely out of the clique. We sat through the meeting holding hands.

When the meeting was over I walked over to Bea and gave her a hug. I told her I loved her. She just smiled that brilliant white smile and walked away. It hurt. But she was able to do what I wasn't until that moment. Let go.

And that was it for Bea and me.

Rich got a few calls from Dan, warning him about working too much. That always bothered Rich. He would hang up saying, "I love what I do. That's how I make money, I work."

Dan always reminded him, "You know what happens when you don't go to meetings." Eventually, those calls stopped too.

So there we were. A couple drunks with no program and no sponsors. We had no accountability, except each other.

But drinking was never a question or a problem.

We just didn't think about drinking.

One day, while driving down beautiful, tree-lined Madrona Avenue, a main road in my new city, I started asking myself questions.

What if I'm not an alcoholic?

What if I don't need a program?

What if I stop thinking about drinking?

What if I shift my focus to how I want to LIVE?

And that's what we did.

We stopped thinking about drinking and focused on creating the lives we wanted to live. It's been over thirteen years. We turned all our attention and focus on building our life together. Daydreaming and doing.

I don't know if I'm an alcoholic.

I haven't had a drop of alcohol since March 3, 2003.

When I don't pick up a drink it's not because I'm afraid I won't be able to stop.

I don't drink because it doesn't fit my lifestyle or support the woman I want to be.

Rich is a little different—he struggled with alcohol for most of his life. He was a "retread" in the program. When I ask him what he attributes his sobriety to, he says: "I think my meds help a lot. I love my life. And I don't feel like shit tomorrow."

He takes a very low dose of anti-depressants that helps stabilize his mood and what he calls, "Race Brain." Race Brain, in case you've never heard of it, is when you can't shut down all the thoughts coming into your mind at once—racing thoughts. It can make a person crazy. It can make a person want to drink.

We talk about going to an AA meeting every now and again. Today, I have no interest. Not that I have anything against AA. I think the twelve steps and the twelve traditions are great. Just like the Bible. It's when the personalities come into play and change the original intention that things get complicated.

I have come to the conclusion that I did what many do with church. I put the power of the program in the people. Not in the twelve steps. Not in the work. Not in the gospel.

And I witnessed a lot of people doing the same in those rooms.

People want to feel connected.

There's a reason for that...

CHAPTER THIRTEEN

CURIOSITY

"The important thing is not to stop questioning. Curiosity has its own reason for existing."

— Albert Einstein

I kept looking for answers to why I stayed sober without struggle. My mom was still drinking at the time. My sister was still drinking, but not as much. However, she was quite dependent on marijuana.

I hadn't heard of anybody having a struggle-free journey.

I submitted that video to Oprah Winfrey Network so that I could find, interview, and highlight different ways women have achieved successful sobriety.

By successful, I mean free from struggle. After all, I couldn't be the only one.

I wanted to help women experience freedom. Freedom to carry on their lives without making their addiction their identity. I wanted women to stop focusing on what was broken and focus on their power to have the life they wanted by making conscious choices. Everyday, small, seemingly meaningless choices that when compounded create your world. (As opposed to the unconscious choices that turn your world upside down...)

As I read and watched everything I could about recovery, at times I became disheartened. Whenever I would get a taste of a new perspective on recovery, it would ultimately lead back to twelve steps. Twelve-step yoga, twelve-step Buddhism, twelve step in churches and twelve step in recovery centers.

I kept bumping into the same theories—that any struggle with alcohol is alcoholism, an incurable disease. That you will spend your life keeping alcohol cravings at bay because they never go away—they're always growing inside you—getting stronger.

And then...

I found a study that revealed what I had suspected and experienced. That community and connection play a powerful role in helping prevent and overcome addiction—and that feelings of isolation are at the root of the addict's need to use.

In this 1960s study that examined whether drugs *cause* addiction, scientists tethered a rat alone in a small cage where the only thing it could do was inject itself with a drug. And it did. Testing with morphine, cocaine, methamphetamine, heroin and more, they were able to demonstrate that the rat would dope himself to death.

Nobody ever went any further with the study. They proved their theory that drugs cause addiction and that an addict will use until death if given an option. That's what they wanted and needed to prove to fuel the War on Drugs campaign.

Then along came Professor Bruce K. Alexander of Simon Fraser University. At first, this made sense to him. But then he started questioning how rats by nature are very social, sexual and industrious creatures—like humans—and to isolate them in a cage with nothing to do would drive them mad. He also thought the soulful and spiritual differences between man and rat should be considered in theories on addiction.

So he and others set up a similar study, and added another component. They caged isolated male and female rats and duplicated the initial results proving rats will inject themselves with drugs until death. Then they built a larger space with wood walls and wood chip flooring. They painted murals on the walls and provided wheels for the rats to run in and cans to hide in. They had male and female rats, so there were soon lots of babies.

They called this Rat Park[7]. It was much more of a

---

[7] http://www.brucekalexander.com/articles-speeches/rat-

normal environment for rats in which they had productive and full lives: work, play, and relationships. They compared the drug use of the isolated rats and the "Rat Park" rats. It became clear that the caged isolated rats consumed great amounts of morphine solution and the rats in Rat Park consumed very little. Even with full access to unlimited amounts of drugs they chose to use minimally.

If the addiction theory held true, once the rats tasted the drug they would keep going back for more and getting high. If drugs were what caused the addiction, they wouldn't have been able to help themselves. But instead the Rat Park rats became involved and connected in their community. You might say they had a sense of purpose.

It's a compelling study. And one of a few that I found in searching for why I never struggled with staying sober.

I felt so grateful for the sense of purpose I began to create way back even before Prince Harming left. I stepped up and took responsibility for everything in

park/148-addiction-the-view-from-rat-park

my life. I looked at all my challenges as stepping stones leading me to better days, baby.

What I took from the study is that I never drank because I had to. I drank because I wanted to numb myself out of my life. There was too much pain, fear and anguish. I couldn't see how to get out. I felt trapped and isolated, just like one of those tethered rats, so I resigned myself to booze my life away. I might have been addicted, but it was an addiction to medicating the pain, not to alcohol.

Maybe you're thinking, "But, Teresa, you walked away from your AA community! Rat Park demonstrates community is vital."

Yes, I did. I was brave enough to walk away from a community that was hurting me. Maybe not intentionally, but I was starting to feel trapped, lonely and abandoned.

If I would have stayed in my small town for the sake of my AA community, I would have gotten drunk. I have no doubt about it. In that town, I felt shame, guilt, regret and trapped. There was no opportunity for personal or professional growth. Nobody in my AA community was as concerned about my sobriety as they were about my past mistakes.

I think that's a lot to bear with just months of sobriety, compounded with all the personal challenges I was already facing alone.

I didn't have a program to lean on. Not one that really supported me. What I learned from the limited time that I was connected to my sponsor was:

- Don't run too much -- you'll overdo it.
- Don't go after what you want – settle for what you got.
- Go ahead and date – but don't fall in love.
- If you don't go to meetings you're going to get drunk.
- You have a monster inside of you that is getting stronger. And it's your disease.
- Your disease is going to tell you that you don't need meetings.
- Your disease will talk you into having a drink.

I was on the edge of a cliff in the middle of a mountain with nowhere to go and the forecast called for a strong wind that was going to push me to my death.

I felt like nose-diving off that cliff and into a bottle of

booze. I couldn't live thinking I had no power over how I wanted to live or who I wanted to be.

I believed my only chance at staying sober was leaving the rooms of AA.

Through AA, I came to understand:

- Alcoholism is genetic.
- It's a progressive disease.
- I'm broken.
- There is no cure.
- AA is the only way.
- Sober is not drinking.
- If I am struggling at all to quit alcohol—I am alcoholic.

None of these common misbeliefs are absolute.

Not one!

How, if I was so broken and diseased, could I resist the urge to drink when I found out I owed the IRS fifty thousand dollars in taxes, filed a three-way bankruptcy leaving me financially destitute, and lost everything, including having the very carpets ripped out of my home?

How could I resist the urge to drink when I'd only

gotten to step four in the twelve steps, then had my sponsor shun me and my AA community dissolve?

How was my grandmother able to quit drinking after a simple request from her youngest daughter? There was no AA meeting, twelve steps or a sponsor to remind her of her disease. She just quit.

How was my mother, who drank to escape fear and to experience a life of her very own (if only temporarily) able to stop drinking without any intervention and remain sober for coming up on ten years?

How could my husband enjoy more than thirteen years of sobriety that he never found in fifteen years of being an AA retread?

How could my sister (who drank right along with me all those years, had a "addiction" to marijuana, and never attended AA or considered herself diseased) one day pray in the shower, *God please release me from this addiction*—and now have over ten years sober without struggle?

And how could her husband, who was terribly addicted to crank for years, by his testimony, lay it at the feet of God and never use again for over nine years?

These stories are just from my inner circle. I have heard and witnessed so many more.

Rich and I concentrated on building our lives. Our community needs were met through establishing true connections with the people in our lives.

Rich found purpose in providing for his family and thrives being loved and cared for. He's rewarded for being one of the best in his field.

I found purpose in providing safe space for women to learn about themselves. I am constantly challenging who I think I am and push myself to try new things. For me, the secret is to keep moving and growing.

Just like with water, I know becoming stagnant breeds fungus and disease.

According to a study released by the Centers for Disease Control and Prevention and the Substance Abuse and Mental Health Services Administration :

Nine in ten adults who drink too much alcohol are not

alcoholics or alcohol dependent.[8]

What if there is more than just normal drinking and alcoholic drinking?

What if many of the people going into the rooms of AA aren't alcoholic?

Today, if someone wants to change their relationship with alcohol, they are typically routed in one direction: Alcoholics Anonymous and the twelve steps. I believe there's a lot of room between "Normal" and "Alcoholic" drinking.

When women come to me, we look at their life as a whole. Not just their drinking.

There's a huge opportunity to change the behavior long before alcoholism develops. And it's likely use and volume of drinking will spike with life challenges and stressful events.

Bill W. and Doctor Bob created Alcoholics Anonymous for people like them. People who could NOT make a decision not to drink because their

---

[8] http://www.cdc.gov/media/releases/2014/p1120-excessive-driniking.html

bodies would go into withdrawal without alcohol.

The twelve traditions say the program is for *anybody* with a desire to quit drinking. But it doesn't say it's for *everybody* with a desire to quit drinking.

Many of the women I talk to and work with can't relate to this level of dependence or addiction. Yet, when drinking is a concern, AA is where they are sent.

After working with a client for only a few weeks she can see she has left her identity, dreams, goals and aspirations somewhere in the past (like I did).

She typically has no idea what she wants. She feels guilt or shame for not being over the moon about her life. She feels selfish. But her spirit has her working orders. And it's thrashing inside trying to get her attention, crying out, "There is more life to live!" And she shuts it down with alcohol.

And what do you suppose happens when she goes to AA?

Even if she's not alcoholic, she's going to believe that monster is in her, too. That she has no power to choose. It's not her fault. It's her disease. And no matter how long she abstains she will never be stronger than the monster (disease).

She might start to believe that if she drinks one drink, she might as well drink twelve. Because she can't help herself. She is powerless.

Our beliefs are powerful.

Back at Bell Rose, when I believed the story of the angry God, filled with anger and vengeance, I believe the congregation was scared. They showed up for every service because they were afraid of angering God. That's a perfect example of using fear to try to control the outcome. Not everybody responds well to fear-based motivation.

I don't.

Not only was I tired about being afraid of drinking, but if I had to live in fear of a monster growing inside of me, I might as well drink. It simply felt like a different prison. I was still trapped. That's not the kind of life I aspired to live.

Freedom is living in pursuit of a life you want. Bit by bit, I got clear on what I wanted, I moved toward it— and went for it. I didn't always get it right, but even getting it wrong moved me forward. And that changed everything. Life is meant to be experienced. We are designed to learn and grow until the end of our time.

WHAT DO YOU WANT?

There is no test to diagnose whether you are alcoholic or not. None. Not even when you're dead, lifeless on the table and slit open from sternum to pelvis, can they unequivocally identify you with alcoholism.

(What they can determine is if you have cirrhosis of the liver and if you have alcohol in your system at the time of death.)

Yet, it's called a disease.

And in many cases alcoholism is likened to diabetes and even cancer.

So if it's a disease, then why can't we test for it?

Why do people have to live believing there's a monster growing inside them? Waiting for them to take just one drink? Could you imagine if you thought of cancer that way? That feels like calling it in— manifesting it.

There are thought leaders and researchers pushing against the popular opinion and beliefs with scientifically-backed studies and research that disprove what's always been sold as truth.

Nobody has a 100-percent accurate answer for those trying to escape the pain of our souls by misusing, overusing or abusing substances, people or things—addiction.

I certainly don't. But there is more than one way. I have a way. To live life Wholly Sober.

It's a personal journey with many turns and twists that are unique to the individual. It takes work—inner work. I could never have imagined how dark my life would get and how much light was possible by choosing to LIVE sober, my way!

There is no easy way to obtain sobriety. Because the pain you're trying to avoid and numb is not easy to face.

If I would have listened to all the naysayers and believed the stories about relapse and retreads and alcoholism, I wouldn't be writing to you today.

I believe in my heart I am so much more than my

struggle with alcohol. That is not my identity.

Candy, the feisty lady in AA, once told me I was on a Pink Cloud. The Pink Cloud *does* exist. For me, it's about putting all my energy and focus on what I want. How I want to live. Who I want to be.

I made a decision thirteen years ago to hop on my Pink Cloud, packed with all my dreams, goals and aspirations and ride it out of the rooms of Alcoholics Anonymous. And even though I experience hard and painful times, my life plans and pursuits, my relationships and my connection to God, pull me through every time—without struggling to remain sober.

I had to shut down all the other voices. Clear my mind of all the "truths" I had been told. Get still. Be patient. And be willing to find my truth in my journey.

I had to be courageous and walk out of the program that offered me community and promised me sobriety and failure if I left.

I had no guarantees that I would remain sober. I learned to listen to my soul and let my spirit lead the way. Thank God I did.

I'm not anti-AA or anti-twelve steps. I believe these are lifesavers for some--not for all.

But I found it's so much more about the person and their life as a whole.

I found it's not about the alcohol.

"For As He Thinks In His Heart, So Is He."

Proverbs 23:7

Conclusion

"Who were you before you the world told you who
you should be?"

–Danielle Laporte

Writing this book has been an extraordinary journey traveling through my life and trusting Spirit to help me select the experiences that I hope and pray will be helpful.

I know what it's like to feel overwhelmed and defeated. I know that feeling of waking up and saying, "I can't believe I drank again."

I know the feeling of being absolutely resolved to quit drinking only to find myself at the corner store to pick up a six-pack. "Just a short six-pack, that's it," I would tell myself.

I know what it's like to wake up and not remember important conversations.

I know what's it's like to lose your *je ne sais quoi.* Your spark. That something special that makes you you.

And I'm not convinced *(and neither are a growing number of experts who have been studying and working in the field of addiction for decades)* if these experiences resonate you're an alcoholic.

I have no way to know. Nobody does really.

What I am convinced of is the label you use to

identify yourself is powerful.

What's now considered alcoholism has vastly expanded. It includes not only those who are hopelessly addicted, down and out, and sweating booze, but also the housewife who has come to rely on wine as a companion in her lonely, disconnected life; the busy, female executive who needs a cocktail or two to stop the assault of racing thoughts; and the single mother who needs a few beers to numb her worry about all the bills that are stacking up.

We have become fooled that we are more connected than ever with our growing number of followers through social media that we collect while sipping a glass of rose'.

Alcohol is the buffer against the pain of dreams tossed aside or the identity assumed because it's "easier" to accept what others think is better or true.

"How could I possibly want anything more?" a new client cried during her consult with me. "I have everything I could ever ask for." She had an emptiness that needed to be filled. Most of us don't identify it as such. We simply drink.

My Spirit called for more. But I had made so many

bad choices it seemed impossible to change.

You CAN change. It may take major decisions. It may not be easy. You may need to change what you *know* or *believe to be true.* You may have painful truths to face.

"I'm too tired to think. Please make it easy for me. Tell me what to do," another client once insisted.

I can't tell you about your desires, dreams and aspirations. Chances are you couldn't tell me about them either, right now. They've been layered over with solutions to immediate problems, the needs of others, obligation to your belief system, your understanding of responsibilities, and so much more.

As long as you numb out and dumb down with alcohol your behavior will only progress and the "need to drink" will sink its teeth in you deeper and deeper.

Perhaps you grow physically dependent. Or perhaps, like me, the more you drink the more you make bad choices and the more overwhelmed you become. It feels impossible to get out. Impossible to change.

It all feels too hard.

You don't have to hit rock bottom to change. That may very well be one of the greatest disadvantages of traditional treatment. When you're not destitute or don't have a story that comes close to comparison, you feel your drinking is not THAT bad and that gives you license to continue drinking as you have.

It's simple, if drinking is slowing you down, holding you back, or keeping you from pursuing the life of your dreams, your drinking is a problem and changes need to be made.

It's about you, the woman. Your life as a whole. Not just about the alcohol.

"To be yourself in a world that is constantly trying to make you something else is the greatest accomplishment."

— Ralph Waldo Emerson

She buried her past

Planted a flower or two,

Said goodbye to the old,

And welcomed the new.

—G [9]

RESOURCES:

Dr. Gabor Mate

http://drgabormate.com/topic/addiction/

Lance M. Dodes, M.D.

http://www.lancedodes.com/what-is-addiction/

Bruke K. Alexander-RAT PARK:
http://www.brucekalexander.com/articles-speeches/rat-park/148-addiction-the-view-from-rat-park

Most excessive drinkers are not alcoholic or dependent.
http://www.cdc.gov/media/releases/2014/p1120-excessive-drinking.html

Teresa Rodden-Video Audition for Oprah Winfrey

http://www.pinkcloudcoaching.com/video-audition-oprah/

About the Author

Teresa Rodden is a certified personal coach, speaker and founder of Pink Cloud Coaching. She offers an innovative approach and proven process that empower women to choose life over alcohol. Her great love and gratitude for God and nature revive her spirit and give her courage to stand for change. With a deep love for her friends and family, she continues to go after life wholly sober. She and her husband, Rich, live in the beautiful Pacific Northwest. This is her first book.

TeresaRodden.com

Teresa@TeresaRodden.com